Alexandra Green

Listening • Speaking • Writing

Skills Booster

3

NEW EDITIONS
English Language Teaching

Contents

Listening

1 Special people
Page 4
- Listening for names and adjectives of quality
  - Multiple matching
- Listening for numbers, qualities, place and spelling of name
  - Complete notes

2 Learning
Page 10
- Listening for times, countries, other information about school activities and subjects
  - Multiple choice pictures
- Listening for information about a school
  - Complete notes

3 Homes
Page 16
- Listening for spelling of address and other information about a house for sale
  - Complete notes
- Listening for locations, numbers and other information about two homes
  - Multiple choice sentence completion

4 Around town
Page 22
- Listening for directions, facilities and means of transport
  - Multiple choice sentence completion
- Listening for days, shops and facilities
  - Multiple matching

5 Having fun
Page 28
- Listening for names and leisure activities
  - Multiple matching
- Listening for days and other information about leisure activities
  - Multiple choice pictures

6 What's on?
Page 34
- Listening for information about a project on TV viewing habits
  - Multiple choice sentence completion
- Listening for location, spelling of name and other information about a film
  - Complete notes

7 Special events
Page 40
- Listening for dates, numbers, times and other information about a special event
  - Complete notes
- Listening for names and special events
  - Multiple matching

8 The natural world
Page 46
- Listening for locations, dates, information about outdoor activities and nature
  - Multiple choice pictures
- Listening for information about oceans
  - Complete notes

9 Shop till you drop!
Page 52
- Listening for names, shops and other ways of shopping
  - Multiple matching
- Listening for times, dates and other information about a shopping complex
  - Multiple choice sentence completion

10 Technology
Page 58
- Listening for information about appearance and function of an object
  - Complete notes
- Listening for information about objects, methods of communication and prices
  - Multiple choice pictures

11 Holidays and travel
Page 64
- Listening for prices, dates, spelling of place and other information about a holiday
  - Complete notes
- Listening for information about holiday location, transport, cost and accommodation
  - Multiple choice sentence completion

12 Ambitions
Page 70
- Listening for a job title, skills, qualifications and qualities required, attractions of job
  - Complete notes
- Listening for names and jobs
  - Multiple matching

Speaking Cards — Page 76
Writing Project pages — Page 83
Word list — Page 107

Speaking	Writing
Describing a special person • Monologue **Comparing celebrities using prompts** • Compare information about why people admire two celebrities	**Writing about a person you admire** • Connecting words • Description (of a person)
Asking and answering questions using prompt cards • Ask and answer questions about schools **Explaining why you are interested in a particular course** • Monologue	**Writing about a stay at a language school** • Relative pronouns • E-mail
Comparing homes using prompts • Compare information about two homes **Describing a home using photos** • Give information for someone to guess the home	**Writing about your home** • Adjective order • Description (of a home)
Asking for and giving directions using word and picture prompts • Ask for and give directions to places in a town **Asking and answering questions using prompt cards** • Ask and answer questions about places	**Writing about a place where you used to go** • Prepositions • E-mail
Comparing leisure activities using prompts • Compare information about two people's favourite activities **Asking and answering questions about leisure activities using question prompts** • Ask questions to guess a leisure activity	**Writing to request information about an activity holiday** • Linking expressions • Letter
Asking and answering questions using prompt cards • Ask and answer questions about a film and a DVD shop **Completing notes and talking about your favourite TV programme** • Monologue	**Writing about a film** • Subheadings • Review
Making suggestions and discussing events for a celebration using pictures • Dialogue **Asking and answering questions about special events using question prompts** • Ask questions to guess a special event	**Writing about a special event** • Phrasal verbs • Narrative (about an event)
Asking and answering questions using prompt cards • Ask and answer questions about national parks **Completing a form and talking about a place you want to go to** • Monologue	**Writing about a national park** • Planning steps • Article
Making suggestions and discussing where to shop and what to buy • Dialogue **Making and responding to a complaint from a customer** • Roleplay using prompts	**Writing about a shopping experience** • Planning questions • Story (with last sentence given)
Asking and answering questions using prompt cards • Ask and answer questions about objects **Describing an object using photos** • Give information for someone to guess the object	**Write about something you have lost** • Infinitive or -ing • Description (of an object)
Discussing two winter holidays using prompts • Dialogue **Completing notes and talking about your ideal holiday** • Monologue	**Writing about a journey you have made** • Clauses (contrast, result, purpose) • Narrative (about a journey)
Asking and answering questions using prompt cards • Ask and answer questions about jobs **Comparing work ambitions using prompts** • Compare information about two people's ambitions	**Replying to a request for advice** • Functional language • E-mail

A Match the people with the descriptions. Then find the adjectives for each person and write them below the pictures.

a ...., ..., ...

b ...., ...

c ...., ...

d ...., ..., ...

e ...., ..., ...

f ...., ..., ...

1 Matthew is a sporty person and he's well-built. He usually dresses casually. ....
2 Tom is always fashionably dressed. He's sociable and very attractive. ....
3 Kelly is always well-dressed. She's reliable and thoughtful and she never forgets birthdays. ....
4 Bill is an elderly man. He's creative and very generous. We spend a lot of time together. ....
5 Sally is chubby. She's quite shy, but she's extremely honest. We share all our secrets. ....
6 Mary is slim. She's the most caring person I've met and she's very patient with children. ....

Now find two adverbs which describe how a person is dressed.

.... and ....

B Listen to two friends talking about people they met on holiday and match the names with the adjectives.

1 Gabby   a good-looking
2 Helen   b patient
3 Steve   c reliable
4 Fred   d shy
5 Natalie   e sociable
6 Harry   f sporty
                   g talented
                   h honest

C Listen to two people talking about a prize and complete the notes.

Children's Helper Prize
When it started: (1) ......nine/9...... years ago
Type of people chosen: caring and (2) ....
Age of winners: over (3) .... years old
Last year's winner: Ellen (4) ....
Type of help given: visit children in (5) ...., tell stories and jokes, play board games
Reason for prize: people will be more (6) .... about children who need help

Speaking

A Think of a special person. Work with your partner to ask and answer these questions.

> How do you know about this person?
> How long have you known this person?
> What makes this person special?
> Which two words describe this person best?

B Complete the chart with the words from the box. Then tell the class about the special person in A using some of these words.

caring   chubby   elderly   generous   good-looking   honest   in his/her early/mid/late teens
in his/her early/mid/late twenties/thirties   middle-aged   patient   reliable   shy   slim
sociable   sporty   talented   talkative   well-built   well-dressed   young

Age	Appearance	Character

C **Jackie Chan and Shakira have both started organisations which help people. Work with your partner and talk about why people admire them. Use the information in the boxes to help you.**

Name:	Jackie Chan
Age:	in his early fifties
Job:	actor
Appearance:	sporty, good-looking
Character:	sociable, generous
Organisation:	Jackie Chan Charitable Foundation
Started:	1988
Where:	Hong Kong, China
Helps:	education for young people, health projects, areas destroyed by earthquakes

Name:	Shakira
Age:	in her early thirties
Job:	singer
Appearance:	short, slim
Character:	talented, caring
Organisation:	Pies Descalzos (Barefoot Foundation)
Started:	1995
Where:	Colombia
Helps:	children in danger

Writing

A Complete the words.

1 Nina likes speaking to people. She's a t _ _ _ _ _ _ _ _ _ person.
2 Our postman always arrives at 9 o'clock. He's very r _ _ _ _ _ _ _ .
3 You can trust an h _ _ _ _ _ friend.
4 Catherine loves giving presents to others. She's g _ _ _ _ _ _ _ _ .
5 Mike loves clothes. He's always f _ _ _ _ _ _ _ _ _ _ dressed.
6 Emily will be a great artist one day. She's a really t _ _ _ _ _ _ _ girl.
7 My uncle is a m _ _ _ _ _ - _ _ _ _ man, but still he enjoys playing football.
8 A school teacher should be p _ _ _ _ _ _ with children.

B Read Barbara's description of a person she admires and write *T* for true or *F* for false.

I've chosen to write about my aunt Erica. I've known her since I was a little girl. She's the best vet in my neighbourhood and I think she's a very special person.

Aunt Erica is in her early forties. She's quite attractive and she's usually well-dressed. She's always been a very shy person, so she's not very talkative. She's one of the most caring people I've ever met and that's why she's always very busy. Everyone goes to her when their pets are ill.

She doesn't have very much free time as she also looks after animals that haven't got homes. Most people in our area know Erica, so if they find a dog in the street, they ring her and take it to her. She can't keep all the pets that people bring, but she takes care of them until she finds a home for them. She's very patient with animals and she's also extremely honest.

I admire Erica most because she shows that she really cares about animals. She doesn't only help them because it's her job.

1 Erica works in Barbara's neighbourhood. ....
2 Barbara's aunt doesn't talk a lot. ....
3 People trust Erica with their pets. ....
4 Erica has got lots of free time. ....
5 Erica keeps the pets she is given. ....
6 Erica helps animals because she loves them. ....

Read again!

In which paragraph does Barbara say

1 what the person does that she admires? ....
2 how old the person is and what she looks like? ....
3 who she's chosen to write about? ....
4 why she admires the person most? ....
5 how long she's known her? ....
6 what the person is like? ....

Complete Barbara's writing plan

Paragraph 1: ....
Paragraph 2: ....
Paragraph 3: ....
Paragraph 4: ....

C Barbara used the words below in her description. Find them and underline them. Then answer the questions.

| and | as | because | but | so |

Which word(s) do we use

1 to add information? ....
2 to show contrast? ....
3 to give reasons? .... and ....
4 to show a result? ....

D Circle the correct words to complete Matt's description.

I've chosen to write about Ed, my basketball coach. He's been my coach for two years **(1)** and / but he's a really special person.

Ed is in his mid twenties and he's very well-built. He's usually dresses casually, **(2)** because / so he doesn't need to wear special clothes to work. He's a sociable person **(3)** and / as he's very talkative with everyone in our basketball club.

Ed is a very patient person, **(4)** but / so he doesn't expect us to be excellent players immediately. He says we have to work hard **(5)** and / but then we'll succeed. I wasn't very good at basketball when I joined the club, **(6)** because / but Ed taught me to play well. He makes us train a lot, **(7)** as / but we haven't got time to be lazy.

I admire Ed most **(8)** and / because he's patient. He has helped me and my friends to become a great team. He's a caring person and we all love him.

Now it's your turn!

1 Use Barbara's writing plan to make notes for your description of a person you admire below.

My writing plan notes

Paragraph 1: ....

Paragraph 2: ....

Paragraph 3: ....

Paragraph 4: ....

2 Now use your writing plan notes to write a description of a person you admire. Then copy your description onto the Writing Project page for Unit 1 on page 83.

2 Learning

Listening

A Complete the school timetable and the note below with the words in the box.

> certificate   chemistry   computer studies
> cookery   course   detention   mark
> PE   pottery   revision

Monday	Tuesday	Wednesday	Thursday	Friday
English	maths	history	maths	English
maths	maths	history	maths	French
maths	(2)	English	English	
LUNCH	LUNCH	LUNCH	LUNCH	LUNCH
(1)	French	French	(4)	(5) ....
French	geography	(3)	history	

1  2  3  4  5

Things to do this week

- Ask about the (6) .... in Spanish at Bigton College.

- Do (7) .... for the maths test. (If I don't, I won't get a good (8) ....!)

- Talk to Mum about school. I had to stay in (9) .... twice this week because I forgot to do my English homework.

- I passed my French exam! Pick up my (10) .... from Miss Collins, the French teacher.

10

Unit 2

B Listen to the six conversations and tick the correct answer for each one.

1 Where is Mandy going to learn Spanish?
- a ITALY ☐
- b SPAIN ☐
- c ENGLAND ✓

2 Why did Jason stay late at school?
- a ☐
- b ☐
- c ☐

3 Where are the students going on their school trip?
- a ☐
- b ☐
- c ☐

4 What time does Helen's lesson end?
- a ☐
- b ☐
- c ☐

5 What subject is Tony not good at?
- a FRENCH ☐
- b GERMAN ☐
- c CHEMISTRY ☐

6 What's new at Lynn's school?
- a ☐
- b ☐
- c ☐

C Listen to Tracy talking about her new school and complete the notes.

Tracy's new school

Name: (1) Green Park Secondary School

Description: modern classrooms, three (2) .... rooms, a large playground, a lake, playing fields

Number of students in each class: twenty to (3) ....

School trips: every (4) ....

Extra activities: cookery, sports, Chinese and (5) ....

Exams: January and (6) ....

A Work with your partner to ask and answer these questions about school. Use the phrases in the boxes to help you.

What do you like most about your school?	The best thing about my school is …
Who's your favourite teacher? Why?	My favourite teacher is … because …
Which subject is the easiest and which one is the most difficult?	The easiest subject is … and the/most difficult subject is …
What is your favourite subject? Why?	My favourite subject is … because …
Where do you go on school trips?	We go on school trips to …
Do you enjoy going on school trips? Why?/Why not?	I enjoy/don't enjoy going on school trips because …

B Ask and answer questions with your partner. Student A should turn to page 76 and look at cards 1A and 2A. Student B should turn to page 79 and look at cards 1B and 2B.

C Think of a course you would like to do and then tell the class about what you have chosen and why you are interested in it. Use the ideas below to help you.

Courses

Chinese

computer studies

cookery

pottery

a new sport

Reasons

creative

exciting

fun

interesting

useful

12

Writing

Unit 2

A Complete the crossword.

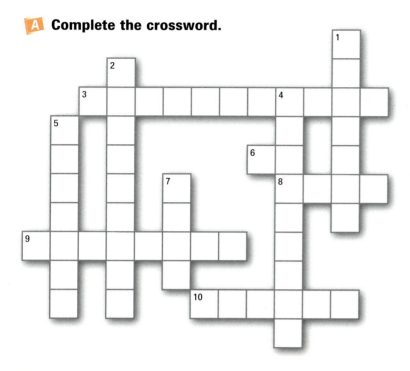

Across

3 This paper shows that you've passed a special exam.
6 You do sports in this lesson.
8 You must get a good one to pass your exam.
9 I have to do this to be ready for my maths test.
10 This is a group of lessons on a subject.

Down

1 Your hands get dirty making things in this lesson.
2 Students stay at school late in this when they are naughty.
4 It's one of the science subjects.
5 It's a tasty subject!
7 We visit different places when we go on this with our teachers.

B Read Annie's e-mail about a course she is doing and answer the questions.

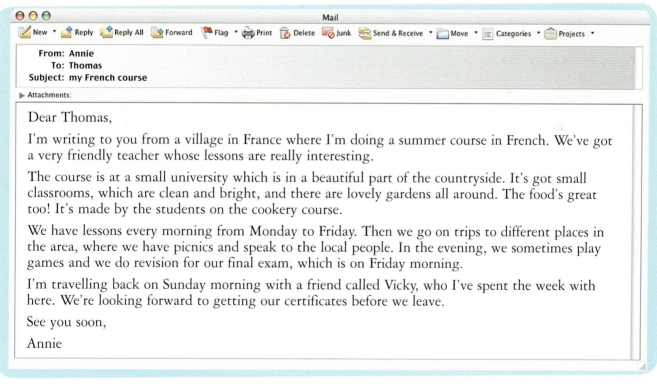

1 Why is Annie in France?
2 What are the lessons like?
3 Where is the university?
4 When does Annie have lessons?
5 What two things does Annie do in the evening?
6 Who is Annie coming back with?

Read again!

In which paragraph does Annie say

1 when she'll be back and who she'll be travelling with? ....
2 where she is, what she's doing and what her teacher is like? ....
3 what the university is like? ....
4 what she's looking forward to? ....
5 what they do each day? ....
6 where the place is and what it is like? ....

Complete Annie's writing plan

Greeting: ....
Paragraph 1: ....
Paragraph 2: ....
Paragraph 3: ....
Paragraph 4: ....
Ending: ....
Sign off: ....

C Annie used the words below in her e-mail. Find them and underline them. Then answer the questions.

> where   which   who   whose

Which word do we use

1 to refer to a person? ....
2 to refer to a place? ....
3 to refer to something? ....
4 to show that something belongs to a person or place? ....

14

D Read Mark's e-mail and complete it with *where, which, who* or *whose*.

From: Mark
To: Sarah
Subject: my German course

Dear Sarah,

I'm writing to you from a town in Germany **(1)** .... I'm on a course learning German. I've got a very funny teacher **(2)** .... lessons are really enjoyable.

The course is at a college **(3)** .... is in the town centre. It's a huge building and it's got a lovely library with lots of computers. There are restaurants, cafés and cinemas nearby, so it's very noisy!

We have lessons in the morning three times a week. In the afternoon, we usually go to the park, **(4)** .... we play football or tennis or go for walks. In the evening, we go to a local restaurant, **(5)** .... has got great food!

I'm flying back in two weeks with my cousin John, **(6)** .... is doing the same course as me. We're both looking forward to getting our certificates at the end of the course.

See you soon,

Mark

Now it's your turn!

1 Imagine that you are at a language school in another country. Use Annie's writing plan to make notes for your e-mail to a friend.

My writing plan notes

Greeting: ....
Paragraph 1: ....
Paragraph 2: ....
Paragraph 3: ....
Paragraph 4: ....
Ending: ....
Sign off: ....

2 Now use your writing plan notes to write an e-mail to a friend about the language school. Then copy your e-mail onto the Writing Project page for Unit 2 on page 85.

A Complete the chart with the words and phrases in the box.

> bungalow   by the sea   chalet   chimney   cottage   cramped   semi-detached house   fence
> fireplace   garage   in the city centre   in the country   in the mountains   in the suburbs   modern
> old-fashioned   roof   spacious   terraced house   tiny

Building	Location	Description	Feature

B Listen to a woman asking for information about a house and complete the advertisement.

FOR SALE

Type of house: (1) .... *detached* ....
Address: 12 (2) .... Place
Downstairs: a (3) .... living room with a fireplace,
                a dining room, a kitchen
Upstairs: 4 bedrooms, (4) ....
Location: in a quiet (5) .... of London
Nearest shops: (6) .... minutes' walk

C Listen to Andrea talking to her teacher about her house and circle a, b or c to complete each sentence.

1 Andrea lives in
   a Randle Road.
   b Hunter's Place.
   c Oakley Park.

2 Andrea has lived in her house for
   a eight years.
   b nine years.
   c fourteen years.

3 Andrea's bedroom
   a is bright pink.
   b has got a view of the garden.
   c is her favourite room.

4 Andrea's best friend
   a lives in the same road as Andrea.
   b is moving house in March.
   c lives two kilometres away from Andrea.

5 Alice's house is different from Andrea's because
   a it doesn't have a dining room.
   b the kitchen is smaller.
   c there is a garage.

6 Alice is going to
   a have a party in the garden.
   b knock down the garage.
   c build a swimming pool.

Speaking

Unit 3

A Work with your partner to ask and answer these questions about your home.

Where do you live?

What kind of house do you live in?

Is it big or small?

Is your house modern or old-fashioned?

How long have you lived there?

Which room do you like best? Why?

B Look at the photos and information about two holiday homes. Discuss the similarities and differences with your partner.

Where:	in Cyprus, by the sea
Type of building:	flat
Outside:	white walls, large windows
Inside:	modern living room, small kitchen, 2 bedrooms, bathroom
Garden/ balcony:	tiny balcony

Where:	in France, in the mountains
Type of building:	wooden chalet
Outside:	big wooden door, small square windows
Inside:	spacious living room with old-fashioned fireplace, small kitchen, 1 bedroom, bathroom
Garden/ balcony:	small garden

C Choose one of the homes below and describe it to your partner. Your partner must guess which home you have chosen.

Unit 3

A Read the descriptions and complete the words.

1 An area which is mostly houses is this.   r _ _ _ _ _ _ _ _ _ _ _
2 Houses which are joined together in a line on the same street.   t _ _ _ _ _ _ _ _
3 It's the opposite of modern.   o _ _ - _ _ _ _ _ _ _ _ _
4 This kind of room or building is big inside.   s _ _ _ _ _ _ _ _
5 This describes something very small.   t _ _ _ _
6 If you put too much furniture in a room, it is like this.   c _ _ _ _ _ _ _
7 This is old furniture which might be expensive.   a _ _ _ _ _ _ _
8 This shape of table has got four straight sides which are all the same size.   s _ _ _ _ _

B Read Pam's description of her home and write T for true or F for false.

My home

My home is in Rise Park, which is a suburb of the city. I've been living here for ten years and I like this area very much. It's a quiet residential area, which has got a big park and a few shops on the main road nearby.

I live in a detached house which has got a small garden at the front and a bigger one at the back. It's got three spacious bedrooms and a bathroom upstairs. Downstairs there's a hall, where we've got a lovely little round Italian glass table and two comfortable red chairs, a living room with a modern fireplace and a large kitchen, with beautiful antique wooden cupboards.

What I like most about my house is my bedroom. I've just decorated it and I've bought a new square green mat, which goes well with my bright yellow curtains. It's a quiet room and I just love the view of the back garden.

1 Pam doesn't live in the city centre.   ....
2 There are no shops near the house.   ....
3 Pam's back garden is smaller than the front one.   ....
4 The bedrooms in Pam's house are big.   ....
5 The fireplace looks old.   ....
6 Pam's can see the garden from her bedroom.   ....

19

Read again!

In which paragraph does Pam say
1 what she likes most about her house? ....
2 what the area is like? ....
3 where she lives? ....
4 what her house is like? ....
5 how long she's been living there? ....

Complete Pam's writing plan

Title: ....
Paragraph 1: ....
....
Paragraph 2: ....
Paragraph 3: ....

C Pam used the words below in her description. Find them and underline them. Then answer the questions.

table   cupboards   mat

What adjectives does Pam use to describe
1 the table? ....
2 the cupboards? ....
3 the mat? ....

In English, adjectives must be used in the right order. The chart below shows the correct order. Write the adjectives Pam uses to describe the table, the cupboards and the mat in the chart.

Opinion	Size	Age	Shape	Colour	Origin	Material	NOUN
							table
							cupboards
							mat

20

D Read Andy's description of his home and put the adjectives below in the correct order to write the missing phrases.

1. garden/big/beautiful
2. roses/red/lovely
3. sofa/modern/blue
4. table/old-fashioned/square
5. chairs/French/antique
6. bookcase/wooden/old

My house

My house is in Sandgate, a suburb of Folkestone. I've been living here since I was born and I love the area. It's a peaceful town by the sea, with a few shops and nice beaches.

I live in a cottage, with a **(1)** .... full of **(2)** .... My house isn't very big and it's quite old, but we've just bought a **(3)** .... for the living room. The kitchen is spacious and it's got an old fireplace. By the window, there's a(n) **(4)** .... where we eat our meals and three **(5)** ....

What I like most about my house is our study. It's tiny but it's got large windows and I can see the garden. There's a(n) **(6)** .... by the door, which used to belong to my grandpa.

Now it's your turn!

1 Use Pam's writing plan to make notes for your description of your home below.

My writing plan notes

Title:	....
Paragraph 1:	....
Paragraph 2:	....
Paragraph 3:	....

2 Now use your writing plan notes to write a description of your home. Then copy your description onto the Writing Project page for Unit 3 on page 87.

4 Around town

 Listening

A Match the words with the numbers on the map of Roxford town centre.

> bowling alley   car park   florist's   newsagent's
> one-way street   pedestrian crossing   petrol station
> roundabout   town hall   traffic lights

1 ....
2 ....
3 ....
4 ....
5 ....
6 ....
7 ....
8 ....
9 ....
10 ....

B Listen to the woman asking a boy for directions and circle a, b or c to complete each sentence.

1 The woman wants to go to the
  a town hall.
  (b) cinema.
  c library.

2 The cinema is two blocks from the
  a bus stop.
  b post office.
  c police station.

3 The woman is going to go
  a on foot.
  b by bike.
  c by bus.

4 She'll turn left at the
  a car park.
  b newsagent's.
  c roundabout.

5 The police station is
  a at the traffic lights.
  b next to the car park.
  c on a one-way street.

6 On Riverside Drive, she'll take the
  a first turning on the right.
  b second turning on the right.
  c second turning on the left.

C Listen to Terry and Wendy talking about where they have to go and match the days with the places.

1 Monday — b
2 Tuesday
3 Wednesday
4 Thursday
5 Friday
6 Saturday

a baker's
b bank
c bowling alley
d cinema
e florist's
f internet café
g town hall
h pedestrian crossing

Speaking

A Work with your partner to ask and answer questions about your neighbourhood. Use the phrases in the boxes to help you.

What is your neighbourhood like?

What facilities are there for entertainment?

What other facilities are there?

Is there anything new in your neighbourhood?

What do you like best about your neighbourhood? Why?

What would you like to change about your neighbourhood? Why?

It's a ... area. There are/aren't many ... in my neighbourhood.

There's a ... and a ... /There are ... and ...

There's a ...

Yes, there's a new ... in my neighbourhood/ No, it's been the same/nothing's changed for years.

The best thing about my neighbourhood is ... / What I like most about my neighbourhood is ...

I would change ... /I think we need a ...

B Work with your partner to ask for and give directions to the places in the town below. Use the phrases in the boxes to help you.

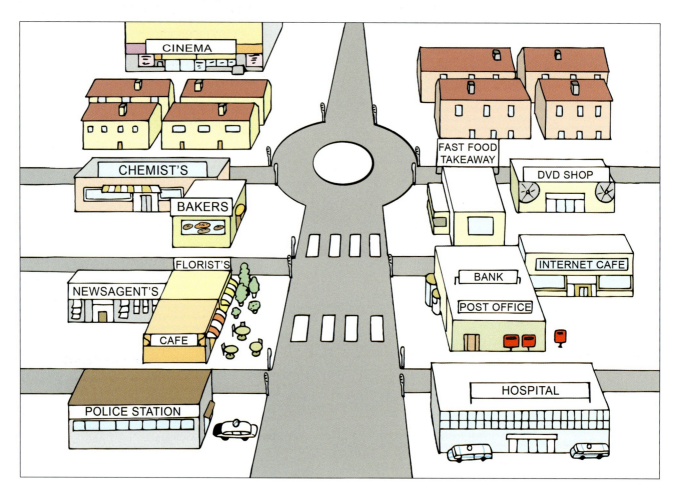

What's the quickest way ... to the ...?

How do I get to the ...?

What's the easiest way to the ...?

Could you tell me the way to the ...?

go round the roundabout

take the first/second/third turning on the right/left

turn right/left at

go straight ahead

cross the road/street at

the ... is on your right/left/straight ahead

1	hospital	→	newsagent's?
2	hospital	→	DVD shop?
3	police station	→	chemist's?
4	fast food takeaway	→	cinema?
5	police station	→	internet café?
6	newsagent's	→	DVD shop?

C Ask and answer questions with your partner. Student A should turn to page 76 and look at cards 3A and 4A. Student B should turn to page 79 and look at cards 3B and 4B.

Writing

A Complete the crossword.

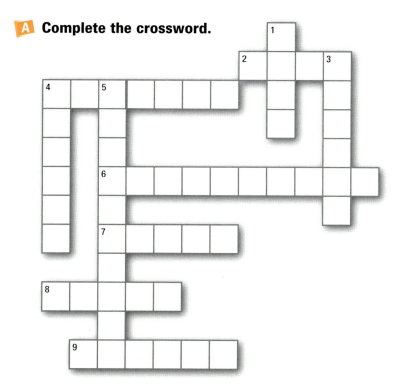

Across

2 There is a bus stop outside the town ....
4 Leave your car in the big .... and you can walk to the shops.
6 We buy newspapers at the ....
7 I go to the bowling .... every Friday after school.
8 There's a lovely park just one .... from my house.
9 You can't turn left into Apple Road because it's a one-way ....

Down

1 Mum thinks I spend too much time in the internet ....
3 Stop your car when the traffic .... are red.
4 The film is on at the .... on Saturday.
5 There are always lots of cars going round the ....

B Read George's e-mail about a place which has changed a lot and answer the questions.

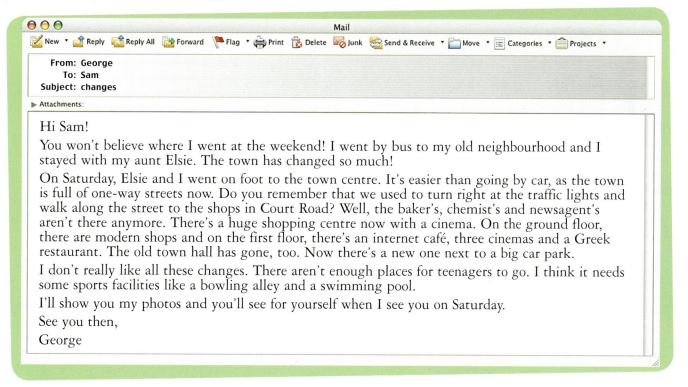

1 Why did George write about his old neighbourhood?
2 Why did George walk to the town centre?
3 Which shops used to be in Court Road?
4 Where are the modern shops in the shopping centre?
5 Which floor is the internet café on?
6 What does George think the town needs?

Read again!

In which paragraph does George say

1. what he thinks about the changes and why? ....
2. what he did on Saturday? ....
3. where he went at the weekend and how he got there? ....
4. how the town has changed? ....
5. when he'll see Sam? ....
6. where he stayed? ....

Complete George's writing plan

Greeting: ....
Paragraph 1: ....
Paragraph 2: ....
....
Paragraph 3: ....
Paragraph 4: ....
Ending: ....
Sign off: ....

C George used the phrases below in his e-mail. Find them and underline them. Then answer the questions.

> at the traffic lights   at the weekend   by bus   by car
> in Court Road   next to a big car park   on foot
> on Saturday   on the first floor   on the ground floor

Which of the prepositional phrases shows us

1. when something was done? ...., ...
2. where something was or where something was done? ...., ...
   ...., ...
   ....
3. how someone travelled? ...., ...
   ....

D **Choose the correct words to complete Alice's e-mail.**

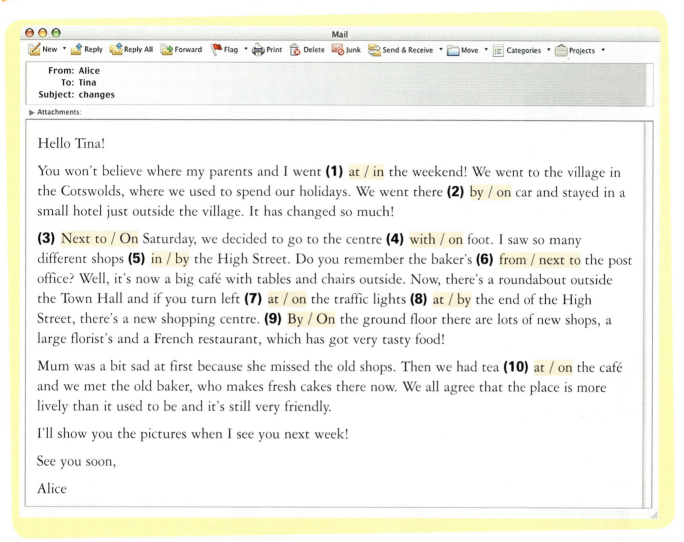

Hello Tina!

You won't believe where my parents and I went **(1)** at / in the weekend! We went to the village in the Cotswolds, where we used to spend our holidays. We went there **(2)** by / on car and stayed in a small hotel just outside the village. It has changed so much!

(3) Next to / On Saturday, we decided to go to the centre **(4)** with / on foot. I saw so many different shops **(5)** in / by the High Street. Do you remember the baker's **(6)** from / next to the post office? Well, it's now a big café with tables and chairs outside. Now, there's a roundabout outside the Town Hall and if you turn left **(7)** at / on the traffic lights **(8)** at / by the end of the High Street, there's a new shopping centre. **(9)** By / On the ground floor there are lots of new shops, a large florist's and a French restaurant, which has got very tasty food!

Mum was a bit sad at first because she missed the old shops. Then we had tea **(10)** at / on the café and we met the old baker, who makes fresh cakes there now. We all agree that the place is more lively than it used to be and it's still very friendly.

I'll show you the pictures when I see you next week!

See you soon,

Alice

Now it's your turn!

1 **Imagine that you went back to a place where you used to go to, which has changed a lot. Use George's writing plan to make notes for your e-mail to a friend.**

My writing plan notes

Greeting: ....
Paragraph 1: ....
Paragraph 2: ....
Paragraph 3: ....
Ending: ....
Sign off: ....

2 **Now use your writing plan notes to write an e-mail to a friend about the place. Then copy your e-mail onto the Writing Project page for Unit 4 on page 89.**

5 Having fun

 Listening

A Match the photos with the words.

 a    b    c

 d    e    f

 g    h    i

 j    k    l

1 ballet ....
2 canoeing ....
3 chess ....
4 cricket ....
5 golf ....
6 hiking ....
7 horseriding ....
8 ice skating ....
9 scuba diving ....
10 skateboarding ....
11 windsurfing ....
12 yoga ....

B Listen to two friends talking about what people did at a summer camp and match the names with the activities.

1 Jack
2 Freddie
3 Donna
4 Nicola
5 Roger
6 Sally

a basketball
b hiking
c ballet
d horseriding
e skateboarding
f cricket
g chess
h windsurfing

28

C Listen to the six conversations and tick the correct answer for each one.

1 What would Sandy do if she had more time?

a ✓   b ☐   c ☐

4 Where do Rose and her sisters go on Wednesdays?

a ☐   b ☐   c ☐

2 Where did Tom go on Saturday?

a ☐   b ☐   c ☐

5 What does Toby find tiring?

a ☐   b ☐   c ☐

3 What did Andy's dad do at the hotel?

a ☐   b ☐   c ☐

6 What's new at the sports centre?

a ☐   b ☐   c ☐

Speaking

A Work with your partner to ask and answer these questions about what you do in your free time.

What do you enjoy doing in your free time?

Which do you like best – indoor or outdoor activities? Why?

What activities do you enjoy doing with your friends?

What activities do you enjoy doing with your family?

Do you have enough free time to do everything you like? Why?/Why not?

If you had more free time, what would you do? Why?

B Look at the information about two people's new activities. Discuss the similarities and differences with your partner.

Anne's new activity

Usual hobbies:	painting, running
Wanted to try:	a water sport
When:	last summer
Where:	at a beach on an island
What:	windsurfing
Who with:	instructor
Liked:	being in the sea, going fast
Didn't like:	falling off

Ted's new activity

Usual hobbies:	cycling, football
Wanted to try:	something creative
When:	last month
Where:	club at school
What:	drama
Who with:	classmates
Liked:	being on stage, acting roles
Didn't like:	forgetting words

C Guess what activity your partner wants to do. Use the words in the box to ask questions.

Indoor/outdoor?
Where play/do?
Alone/friends/team?
Coach/instructor?
Equipment?
How play/do?

Unit 5

A Read the advertisement and complete the words.

New leisure and Sports complex

Water sports: swimming, **(1)** c _____, **(2)** s _____ d _____, **(3)** w _____
Dance studio: **(4)** b _____, **(5)** h _ _ h _ _ (Studio also used for **(6)** y ___ classes.)
Team sports: volleyball, **(7)** c _____, basketball
Indoor activities: **(8)** t _____ t _____, badminton
Outdoor trips: **(9)** h _____ and **(10)** h _____

B Read Dan's letter about a summer camp and write *T* for true or *F* for false.

Dear Anthony,

How are you? I hope you're well. I'm sorry I haven't written for so long, but I've been busy with exams, which have just finished. I'm writing to ask you about the summer camp you went to last year. I'd like to go with you this year.

First of all, can you tell me something about the activities? You know I like five-a-side football, but I'd also like to try something new – maybe horseriding and bowling. Would I be able to do either of these? I know you play chess a lot, but I'm not very keen on that! Can you also tell me what we can do near the camp? Last year, you went cycling and hiking in the hills. That sounds exciting! Did you go to a different place every day and could you choose which trips to go on?

What's more, please tell me how we'll spend the evenings. Can we just relax and play games or read? I'd like that. Are there any computers or televisions we can use? Should I bring some of my board games along or do they have enough to do there?

Finally, when do I have to book a place and how much does it cost? I'd love to come with you this year, so please write back soon and I can arrange it.

Thanks a lot.

Yours,

Dan

1 Dan is doing exams now. ....
2 Anthony has already been to this summer camp. ....
3 Dan wants to do new activities. ....
4 Anthony did outdoor activities. ....
5 Dan has got some board games. ....
6 Dan knows how much the camp costs. ....

Read again!

In which paragraph does Dan

1. ask his friend to write back soon? ....
2. ask what activities he can do at the camp during the day? ....
3. say why he's writing? ....
4. ask for information about what he can do in the evenings? ....
5. ask for information about what he can do near the camp? ....
6. ask when he has to book and how much it costs? ....

Complete Dan's writing plan.

Greeting: ....
Paragraph 1: ....
Paragraph 2: ....
Paragraph 3: ....
Paragraph 4: ....
....
Ending: ....
Sign off: ....

C Dan used the words below in his letter. Find them and underline them. Then answer the questions.

> Can you also tell me   Finally,
> please write back soon   First of all,
> I'm writing to ask you about   What's more,

Which words do we use

1. to give a reason for writing? ....
2. to say what information you'd like to know first? ....
3. to ask for more information? ....,
   ....
4. to end the letter? ....
5. ask for a reply? ....

D Read Tina's letter about activities at a holiday resort and complete it with the words from C.

Dear Debbie,

How are you? I hope you're well. I'm sorry I haven't written for so long, but I've been very busy. Now, it's nearly summer and **(1)** .... the holiday resort you stayed at last year. My parents and I are interested in going somewhere where there's something for all three of us to do and I'd just like to know a few things.

(2) .... can you tell me about the activities? Dad enjoys scuba diving and we'd all like to go horseriding. As you know, I like swimming in the sea and windsurfing too. Would we be able to do any of these activities there? **(3)** .... what else we can do near the resort? Are there trips to other places? What about other kinds of sports?

(4) .... I'd like to know how we can spend the evenings. Are there any competitions in the hotel? You mentioned dancing and bowling when we spoke. What kind of dancing was there? Was there a bowling alley at the hotel or did you go to the nearest town?

(5) .... when do we have to book a place and how much does it cost? We'd love to go as it sounds perfect for us, so **(6)** .... and we can make arrangements.

Thanks a lot.

Love,

Tina

Now it's your turn!

1 Use Dan's writing plan to make notes for your letter to a friend asking for information about an activity holiday below.

My writing plan notes

Greeting: ....
Paragraph 1: ....
Paragraph 2: ....
Paragraph 3: ....
Paragraph 4: ....
Ending: ....
Sign off: ....

2 Now use your writing plan notes to write a letter asking for information about an activity holiday. Then copy your letter onto the Writing Project page for Unit 5 on page 91.

33

6 What's on?

A Complete the chart below with words and phrases from the TV guide.

TV Guide

TOP 3 FILMS

Honey
The funniest comedy ever with an excellent cast and a surprising plot!

The Hope Kids
A family drama with a predictable plot, a strong cast and a happy ending.

Crash
A thriller with a few famous actors, an action-packed plot and a sad ending.

TOP 3 TV PROGRAMMES

Who's watching?
A reality show puts a group of unknown characters in an exotic location with some interesting action.

Island Life
Don't miss this fascinating documentary about the unusual lives of ordinary people living on small islands around the world.

Roslyn Place
This week sees the twenty-fifth episode of this soap opera with a talented cast, but a boring storyline.

Type of film/programme	Describing the actors	Describing what happens
....	....	....
....	....	....
....	....	....
....	....	....
....	....	....
....	....	....

B Listen to Kay talking to her teacher about her school project and circle a, b or c to complete each sentence.

1 Kay interviewed most of the students
   a at school.
   b in video clubs.
   c at internet cafés.

2 Teenagers who are the same age as Kay prefer
   a serials films.
   b films.
   c soap operas.

3 Older teenage boys watch more
   a adventure.
   b thrillers.
   c comedies.

4 Girls like films with an ending that's
   a surprising.
   b happy.
   c sad.

5 The number of students who think reality shows are predictable is
   a 15.
   b 25.
   c 50.

6 Students between fifteen and eighteen would like to see more
   a documentaries.
   b music shows.
   c sports programmes.

C Listen to an actor talking about his latest film and complete the notes.

In Jake's Footsteps

Filmed in: the mountains of (1) Canada

Director: Joe (2) ....

Type of film: (3) .... adventure

Plot: easy to follow with a (4) ....

Cast: mainly young (5) .... actors

In cinemas: from (6) .... June

A Work with your partner to ask and answer these questions about TV programmes and the cinema. Use the phrases in the boxes to help you.

What kind of films do you like watching on TV or at the cinema?

Do you go to the cinema often? Why?/Why not?

How often do you rent films from a DVD club?

Who decides what films or programmes you will watch?

What do you think of TV programmes in your country?

What types of programmes would you like to see more of on TV?

I'm keen on ... /I really enjoy ...

Yes, - about once a week/month ... / No, because ...

Two or three times a week/month/ year/Not often/Never because ...

My ... usually decides because ... / I do because ...

I think they are ... in general.

I'd definitely like to see more ...

B Ask and answer questions with your partner. Student A should turn to page 77 and look at cards 5A and 6A. Student B should turn to page 80 and look at cards 5B and 6B.

C Complete the notes about your favourite TV programme. Then tell the class about it.

Name of programme: ....

Type of programme: ....

Which day: ....

Plot: ....

Cast: ....

Why I like it: ....

# Writing

 Unit 6

A Read what the newspapers say about the new TV programmes and complete words.

1. A great c _ _ _ _ _ ! It made us laugh a lot!
2. It's the best s _ _ _ o _ _ _ _ in the world!
3. A new r _ _ _ _ _ _ _ s _ _ _ that shows the lives of different celebrities at home.
4. The p _ _ _ is predictable, but the film is worth watching.
5. A new police d _ _ _ _ about a dog which helps to solve a mystery.
6. Most of the film is predictable, though the ending is s _ _ _ _ _ _ _ _ _
7. A different kind of s _ _ _ _ _ _ f _ _ _ _ _ _ film that doesn't just take you to space and back.
8. Thanks to the brilliant c _ _ _ of new actors, this adventure film is great!

B Read Vivienne's film review and answer the questions.

Summer Surprise starring John Fisher and Kate Wyles

The film
Summer Surprise is a romantic comedy about two students who are travelling after they've graduated from university. Their last stop is a small fishing village in southern Italy, where most of the film is set.

The story
The stars of the film, John Fisher and Kate Wyles, team up with two new actors, Nancy Stokes and Matt Keane. During a trip around Europe, Jane and Katie (Wyles and Stokes) decide to stay in Italy for the summer. They fall in love with the village and with Joe and Luca (Fisher and Keane), who play the Italians. Six months later, summer has passed and the two girls are still enjoying spaghetti and cappuccino in the village square.

The good and the bad
Thanks to the cast, the film is a great success. There are some very funny scenes, which make the film even more entertaining. The plot is easy to follow, but quite predictable, just like the ending.

My advice
If you want to relax at the cinema and have a good laugh, go and watch this film. Don't expect a 'summer surprise' though. There aren't any surprises in this film.

1. What kind of film is *Summer Surprise*? ....
2. Which two main actors star in the film? ....
3. How long do the two girls plan to stay in Italy? ....
4. Why do the girls end up staying? ....
5. Why is the film a great success? ....
6. What does Vivienne say about the ending? ....

Read again!

In which paragraph does Vivienne say
1. whether she thinks the film is worth watching? ....
2. who plays in the film? ....
3. what the plot is? ....
4. what type of film it is? ....
5. where it is set? ....
6. what is good or bad about the film? ....

Complete Vivienne's writing plan.

Title: ....
Paragraph 1: ....
....
Paragraph 2: ....
Paragraph 3: ....
Paragraph 4: ....

C Vivienne used the subheadings below to make her film review more interesting, and so the reader knows exactly what information will be in each paragraph.

1st paragraph: The film
2nd paragraph: The story
3rd paragraph: The good and the bad
4th paragraph: My advice

Subheadings can also be questions. Which paragraphs match these new subheadings?

1. What's the plot? ....
2. What's good and what's bad? ....
3. Is it worth seeing? ....
4. What is Summer Surprise? ....

D The paragraphs from Jim's review of the new film *Shake* are in the wrong order. Put the paragraphs in the correct order, then write the correct questions from C as subheadings.

Shake
starring Tom Karr and Melanie Sykes

....

a ☐ It all starts when Rob (Karr) and his sister Annie (Sykes) see a bright light coming from the aeroplane when they're walking their dog one night. Every time they get closer to the plane, the light disappears. They even take their friends to see this strange light and they all decide that the plane used to be a spaceship and that every night the aliens come back to it.

....

b ☐ It's not the best science-fiction film, but if you like the idea of aliens and spaceships and you don't have anything better to do, go and see the film.

....

c ☐ The group of young actors is brilliant, but the plot suddenly disappears, just like the light, and the ending isn't at all surprising.

....

d ☐ *Shake* is a science-fiction film about two children who find an old aeroplane in the middle of a field, where most of the film is set. They believe that it is actually a spaceship from another planet.

Now it's your turn!

1 Use Vivienne's writing plan to make notes for your film review.

My writing plan notes

Heading: ....
Paragraph 1: ....
Paragraph 2: ....
Paragraph 3: ....
Paragraph 4: ....

2 Now use your writing plan notes to write a film review. Then copy your review onto the Writing Project page for Unit 6 on page 93.

7 Special events

Listening

A Match the photos with the words.

a
b
c
d
e
f
g
h

1 carnival procession ....
2 charity concert ....
3 Guy Fawkes Night ....
4 The London Marathon ....
5 The Olympic Games ....
6 The World Cup ....
7 film festival ....
8 fancy-dress party ....

B Listen to a tourist guide telling a tourist about a special event and complete the notes.

THE LONDON MARATHON

1st London Marathon: **(1)** ......29th...... March 1981

People taking part this year: more than **(2)** .... people

Start: close to **(3)** .... Park

Starting time: between **(4)** .... and 10 am

Some people wear: **(5)** .... costumes

Reasons people run: to raise money for **(6)** .... and for fun

Unit 7

C Listen to two friends talking about school projects and match the names with the special events.

1 Alice   a carnival

2 Bob   b Guy Fawkes Night

3 Frank   c fancy-dress party

4 Louise   d film festival

5 James   e fireworks display

6 Cindy   f The Olympic Games

               g charity TV programme

               h The World Cup

(1 — g)

Speaking

A Think of a special event you have been to. Work with your partner to ask and answer these questions about it.

What kind of special event was it?

When did it take place?

Where did it take place?

Who did you go with?

What happened?

What did you enjoy most about it?

Is there another kind of special event you would like to take part in? What is it? Why would you like to take part in it?

B Imagine that you are helping to plan a celebration in your town. Work with your partner and decide which of these special events would be the most interesting, or choose another event that you can think of. Use the phrases in the boxes to help you.

a    b    c

d    e    f

How about ...?

What about ...?

What do you think of ...?

Let's have a ...

I think ... is a great idea ... because ...

That's a good idea!

Yes, I agree.

No, I don't agree/I don't think so ... because

I think ... would be better/more fun ... because ...

C Guess what special event your partner wants to go to. Use the words in the box to ask questions.

Where?

When?

Fancy dress?

Dancing?

Any sports?

Fireworks?

Celebrities?

A Complete the crossword.

Across

2 All football players dream of playing in the .... Cup.
5 Which country won the most gold medals in the last Olympic ....
7 There'll be lots of famous actors at the film ....
8 Would you like to .... in a special event?
9 All the runners were wearing ....
10 How many people will run in the London .... this year?

Down

1 The bands raised a lot of money for charity at the ....
3 The evening ended with a fantastic fireworks ....
4 We saw some wonderful costumes in the .... procession.
6 .... is another word for a famous person.

B Read Katy's narrative about a special event and write *T* for true or *F* for false.

Last year, my family and I went to Venice, one of the most amazing places I've ever visited. In February every year, thousands of visitors from all over the world travel there to take part in the spectacular carnival.

As soon as we arrived at our hotel, we put on our costumes and set out on our adventure. As we walked through the busy streets, we couldn't believe our eyes! The tiny streets and main square were full of people wearing amazing costumes! While we were walking through the crowded streets, we noticed bands playing different kinds of music and people singing and dancing all around us. The atmosphere was incredible. Dad was taking some pictures and suddenly a tall man came up to us and asked if he could take our picture. We were all surprised and wondered why he wanted a photo of us. He carried on talking to us and Dad explained that we had to leave. At that moment, the man took off his mask and told us that we had three of the best costumes he had seen that day. He invited us to take part in the final fancy-dress competition.

Later on, we had lunch in one of the local restaurants. Then we decided to go back and relax at our hotel. We were happy and very excited. We were looking forward to the evening and we didn't want to be too tired.

The celebration that night was out of this world! There were dancers, acrobats and actors performing and entertaining the crowds in a beautiful outdoor theatre. We went on stage with thirty other people in fancy dress so that the best costume could be chosen. In the end, we didn't win a prize, but this was one of the most exciting days of my life!

1 The carnival in Venice takes place once a year. ....
2 Katy and her parents walked around Venice in fancy dress. ....
3 Katy's dad wanted to take a picture of a tall man. ....
4 The tall man took off his mask when Katy's dad said he wanted to leave. ....
5 Katy and her family relaxed in a local restaurant. ....
6 In the end, everyone won a prize. ....

Read again!

In which paragraph does Katy

1. describe what they did when they arrived at their hotel? ....
2. say what happened finally? ....
3. say where she visited? ....
4. say when she went? ....
5. say who she went with? ....
6. describe what they did and how they felt before they went out in the evening? ....
7. describe what she saw and heard around her? ....

Complete Katy's writing plan

Paragraph 1: ....
Paragraph 2: ....
Paragraph 3: ....
Paragraph 4: ....

C Katy used the phrasal verbs below in her narrative. Find them and underline them. Then match them with their meaning.

1. carry on   a approach
2. come up to   b continue
3. put on   c participate in
4. set out   d dress in something
5. take part in   e remove
6. take off   f start a journey

D Read Toby's narrative about a special event and complete it with the phrasal verbs from C in the correct form.

A month ago, I went to visit my cousin in Lewes, east Sussex, where Guy Fawkes Night is a huge tradition. In Lewes, they don't just put the Guy on the bonfire and enjoy fireworks. People wear fancy-dress costumes and walk around the streets. I couldn't wait to **(1)** .... this magnificent celebration.

As soon as I arrived at my cousin's house, we **(2)** .... our fancy dress costumes and **(3)** .... on our walk to the town centre. The atmosphere was spectacular. While we were walking along the street, a man in an unusual costume **(4)** .... us and started talking. I was a bit scared, so I **(5)** .... walking. Suddenly, he jumped in front of me and **(6)** .... his mask. At that moment, I realised that it was my uncle Joe. I couldn't believe my eyes!

Later on, we walked along the crowded streets, full of people in magnificent costumes. Then we went to watch a fancy-dress competition at the town hall, where they picked the best costume. Uncle Joe won second prize for his costume and we were all proud of him. It was an amazing event and we had a very good time.

In the end, we went outside and watched a fantastic fireworks display which was out of this world. This was one of the most exciting nights of my life!

Now it's your turn!

1 Imagine you have taken part in a special event. Use Katy's writing plan to make notes for your narrative about it.

My writing plan notes

Paragraph 1: ....
Paragraph 2: ....
Paragraph 3: ....
Paragraph 4: ....

2 Now use your writing plan notes to write a narrative about a special event. Then copy your narrative onto the Writing Project page for Unit 7 on page 95.

8 The natural world

 Listening

A Match the words with the descriptions.

1 deserts

2 glaciers

3 oceans

4 peaks

5 rainforests

6 volcanos

a There are around 1,500 active ones in the world and the largest one is Mauna Loa, in Hawaii. They look like mountains and they can be active, dormant or extinct. When they erupt, fire, smoke and lava come out of them.

b They cover about 70% of the surface of the Earth. The two largest ones are the Pacific and the Atlantic.

c These are warm, wet forests which are the natural habitat of many plants and animals. They can be found in South America, West Africa, Australia, South India and South-East Asia.

d There are very dry areas, with very hot days and cold nights, where it does not rain often. There are many plants here which don't need much water and there are animals, which sleep during the day and come out at night.

e These are the tops of mountains. You have to climb up the mountain slopes to reach these points.

f There are a huge areas of ice which move like slow rivers. They are found in Antarctica and in very cold or high places.

46

B Listen to the six conversations and tick the correct answer for each one.

1 Which part of the world was the documentary about?

- a ☐ Asia
- b ☐ Africa
- c ✓ Antarctica

2 What was the most exciting thing about Mandy's holiday?

- a ☐
- b ☐
- c ☐

3 What did Gordon do on the last day of his trip?

- a ☐
- b ☐
- c ☐

4 What will Annie's school project be about?

- a ☐
- b ☐
- c ☐

5 What date does the magazine come out every month?

- a ☐ 13th
- b ☐ 15th
- c ☐ 30th

6 Where is Uncle Ted now?

- a ☐
- b ☐
- c ☐

C Listen to a geography teacher talking about oceans and complete the notes.

Oceans

- Oceans cover: 3/4 of the Earth's **(1)** surface
- Number of oceans: **(2)** ....
- Largest ocean: **(3)** .... Ocean
- Coldest ocean: **(4)** .... Ocean
- Important because:
  - control the **(5)** .... and the temperature on Earth
  - home to many animals and **(6)** ....

A Work with your partner to ask and answer these questions about the natural world.

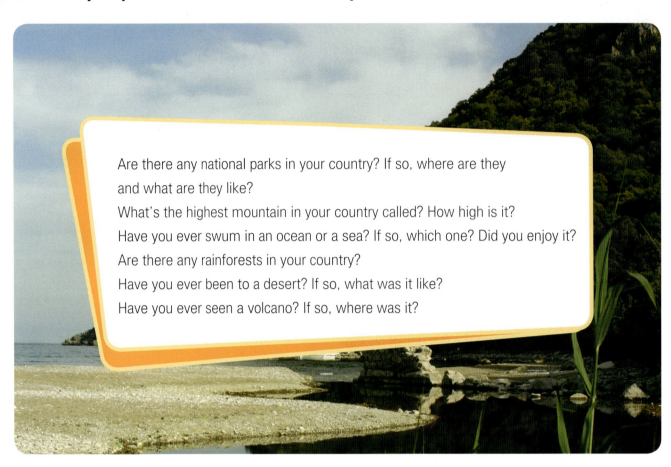

Are there any national parks in your country? If so, where are they and what are they like?

What's the highest mountain in your country called? How high is it?

Have you ever swum in an ocean or a sea? If so, which one? Did you enjoy it?

Are there any rainforests in your country?

Have you ever been to a desert? If so, what was it like?

Have you ever seen a volcano? If so, where was it?

B Ask and answer questions with your partner. Student A should turn to page 77 and look at cards 7A and 8A. Student B should turn to page 80 and look at cards 7B and 8B.

C Imagine that you have won a competition in a magazine called *The Natural World*. Complete the form about the place you want to go to. Then tell the class about it.

Where: ....

Why: ....

What things you'd like to see: ....

What wldlife you'd like to see: ....

What you'd like to do: ....

Writing

A Complete the crossword.

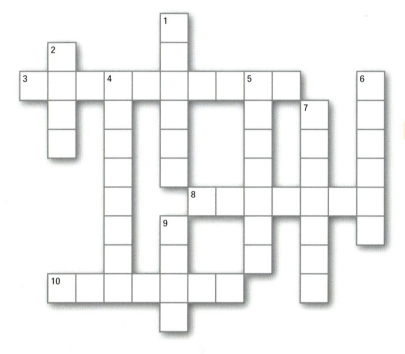

Across

3 Every .... is important to us, so we mustn't cut trees there.
8 A .... is like a huge river of ice.
10 Fire and lava comes out of a .... when it erupts.

Down

1 You can go skiing on the .... of the mountain.
2 We went on a guided ... through the forest.
4 There is a lot of wildlife to see in this .... park.
5 Oceans cover a huge part of the .... of Earth.
6 In a ...., there isn't much water.
7 The .... is the biggest ocean in the world.
9 It took five days to climb to the .... of Kilimanjaro.

B Read Duncan's article about the Cairngorms National Park and answer the questions.

A trip to natural relaxation

Are you looking for a peaceful break in a beautiful setting? If you are, come and visit the Cairngorms National Park, which is Britain's largest national park. It is located in the north of Scotland and covers an area of 3,800 square kilometres.

The park is amazing. There are huge mountain peaks, which are actually extinct volcanoes, together with magnificent rivers, calm lakes and lovely plants. While you're walking around, you'll see animals and birds everywhere.

At Cairngorms, there are plenty of activities, too. You can enjoy mountain biking, climbing or canoeing in all seasons in this wonderful environment. If you want something more relaxing, you can go on a guided walk in the forests, where you'll learn about the beautiful plants and animals. People who are interested in birds can enjoy bird watching and, if you are lucky, you might even see a golden eagle. Winter visitors can also go skiing.

Every year, thousands of visitors enjoy these peaceful surroundings. Why don't you join them?

1 Where is the national park? ....
2 What size is the park? ....
3 What can you see when you walk around the park? ....
4 What activities can you enjoy at any time of the year? ....
5 What can you do if you like birds? ....
6 What winter sport can you do? ....

Read again!

In which paragraph(s) does Duncan

1. say what activities you can do there? ....
2. say what you can see? ....
3. say what the area is like? ....
4. say where the park is? ....
5. ask a question? ...., ...

Complete Duncan's writing plan

Title: ....
Paragraph 1: ....
Paragraph 2: ....
Paragraph 3: ....
Paragraph 4: ....

C Duncan used the following steps to write his article.

Steps	What Duncan wrote
1 Use a title that will make readers want to read on.	A trip into natural relaxation
2 Ask a question to make the introduction more interesting.	Are you looking for a peaceful break in a beautiful setting?
3 Tell the readers what they can see there.	While you're walking around …
4 Tell the readers about the activities available	At Cairngorms, there are plenty of activities …
5 Give the reader a choice.	If you want something more relaxing …
6 End your article in a way that will make the reader want to know more.	Why don't you join them?

Now match these phrases and sentences with the steps above.

a If you want some action … ....
b Would you like to enjoy an adventure in a beautiful park on the Pacific Ocean? ....
c What are you waiting for? ....
d While you explore this area … ....
e Adventure in a natural environment ....
f For something more relaxing … ....

D Read Irene's article about the Pacific Rim National Park and complete it with the phrases and sentences from C.

(1) ....

(2) .... If so, visit the Pacific Rim National Park, located in British Columbia, Canada.

This huge national park has got lovely beaches together with thick rainforests and mountains. There are lakes and long rivers, which used to be glaciers, everywhere. (3) .... you'll see different kinds of birds, deer, wolves and bears and the ocean is full of many kinds of whales and fish.

(4) ...., you can try surfing, diving, kayaking or canoeing. (5) ...., you can go bird watching or just enjoy a long walk along the beach and admire the shells. You might be lucky enough to see a whale, too.

There's so much to discover and enjoy. (6) ....

Now it's your turn!

1 Use Duncan's writing plan to make notes for your article about a national park in your country.

My writing plan notes

Title: ....
Paragraph 1: ....
Paragraph 2: ....
Paragraph 3: ....
Paragraph 4: ....

2 Now use your writing plan notes to write an article about a national park. Then copy your article onto the Writing Project page for Unit 8 on page 97.

9 Shop till you drop!

 Listening

A Complete the advertisements.

> boutique   catalogue   department store   discount
> greengrocer's   jeweller's   sales   shopping complex

(1) ....
20% off
gold & silver watches.
Offer ends on the
3rd September

Bea's
(2) ....
Special offer on
fantastic designer
clothes for men
& women!

Charley's
(3) ....
Order quality clothes
and shoes, delivered
straight to your door.
30%
(4) ....
if you order this week!

(5) ....
start this Monday at
Gateman's four-storey
(6) ....
Clothes, shoes and perfumes
at bargain prices!

(7) **New local**
....
Fresh fruit & vegetables
at low prices. Come and
try us out!

Huge
(8) ....
4 km outside the city
centre. Thirty different
kinds of shops, with
restaurants and cinemas
all under one roof.
Free parking.

B Listen to two friends talking about where people bought presents for Danielle and match the names with the places.

1 Jack
2 Billy
3 Graham
4 Lynne
5 Richard
6 Sally

a boutique
b catalogue
c department store
d greengrocer's
e clothes shop
f jeweller's
g web site
h newsagent's

C Listen to two friends talking about a new shopping complex and circle a, b or c to complete each sentence.

1 The number of people who shop in the High Street is
   a lower than it used to be.
   b higher than it used to be. *(circled)*
   c the same as it used to be.

2 The quickest way to get to the shopping complex is
   a by car.
   b by train.
   c by bus.

3 The shops there are open from
   a 9 am till 5.30 pm.
   b 9 am till 8 pm.
   c 9 am till 7 pm.

4 In the complex, there are two
   a snack bars.
   b cinemas.
   c restaurants.

5 There's a two-storey
   a music shop.
   b internet café.
   c department store.

6 The sales start
   a next Monday.
   b on Monday 27th.
   c on Monday 13th.

A Work with your partner to ask and answer these questions about shopping.

> When do you usually go shopping? Who with?
> What kinds of shops are in your town/city/village?
> Where do you go to buy presents?
> Where does your family buy fruit and vegetables?
> Have you ever bought anything online or from a catalogue?
> If so, what did you buy?

B Imagine that you and your friend want to buy a present for a classmate. Discuss where to buy the present from and what to buy. Use the phrases in the box to help you.

1  2  3  4  5

> I think we should go to ...
> We could try ...
> How about ...?
> What about ...?
> That's a great idea./I don't think so.
> I agree with you./I don't agree with you.

C Work in pairs. One of you will be Student A and the other will be Student B. Write a dialogue and then act it out in front of the class. Use the phrases in the box to help you.

Student A

The problem

You ordered a shirt from a catalogue and when it came through the post, it wasn't the size you wanted. You had ordered medium and on the inside of the shirt it said 'medium', but it looked too small. You tried it on to see if it fitted you, but the moment you put it on, it tore.

What you want:
- to send it back.
- to get your money back or to get a new shirt in a larger size.

Student B

The problem

You work for the catalogue and you have to explain to the customer that you can't give him his money back because the shirt has been torn.

What you can do:
- tell the customer to order another shirt, in a bigger size.
- give the customer a 20% discount on the new shirt.

I was very surprised to see that …	I'm sorry but …
Please could you …	I'm afraid I can't …
I'd be grateful if you could …	Why don't you …?
I'd like you to …	How about …?
	The only thing I can do is …

Writing

Unit 9

A Complete the chart to show where you can buy these things.

biscuits bread cake cucumber dress earrings necklace pear
pie potatoes ring skirt tights trousers watch watermelon

Baker's	Boutique	Greengrocer's	Jeweller's
....	....	....	....
....	....	....	....
....	....	....	....
....	....	....	....

B Arthur wrote a story which ends with the words *'It was the most embarrassing day of my life!'* Read his story and write *T* for true or *F* for false.

Three weeks ago, we got a leaflet in the post about a new department store in our town. There was a special offer with about 25% off everything in the shop. I kept the leaflet and yesterday Mum and I decided to go.

When we got to the department store, we couldn't believe how big it was. I was so excited. Mum saw a lovely dress for £40, I found a pair of shoes for the same price and we got three pairs of socks for Dad, which were £3 a pair on the leaflet. We chose a lovely leather handbag for my aunt's birthday. The quality was great and the price was high, but we thought it would be a bargain with the discount.

Mum and I had filled up our basket and we went to pay. We were really happy with how much we'd bought for the low price we would pay. Well, that's what we thought.

In the end, the bill came to £150 and Mum had just £120 in her purse! I told Mum not to worry and I showed the leaflet to the shop assistant with the discounts on everything we had bought. She pointed to the top, where 'Shop this week' was written and that was three weeks ago. I didn't know what to do. It was the most embarrassing day of my life!

1 Arthur went shopping three weeks ago. ....
2 Arthur's shoes cost £40. ....
3 The leaflet mentioned socks at £3 a pair. ....
4 The handbag was expensive without the discount. ....
5 Arthur and his mum paid just £120. ....
6 The shop assistant gave Arthur the discount when he showed her the leaflet. ....

Read again!

In which paragraph does Arthur say

1. what happened in the end? ....
2. when and how the whole story started? ....
3. what the shop was like and what they wanted to buy? ....
4. what happened when they went to pay? ....
5. how they felt when they had filled their basket? ....

Complete Arthur's writing plan

Paragraph 1: ....
Paragraph 2: ....
Paragraph 3: ....
Paragraph 4: ....

C Before Arthur wrote his story he asked himself some questions to help him make his plan.

Who is main character?
What is the story about?
When did it happen?
Where did it happen?
How did the people feel at the beginning of the story?
How did the story develop?
Why was it the most embarrassing day of his life?

Before you start writing a story, you should

- think of a good idea
- think about who the main character is, when the story took place, and where it took place
- think about a good ending that fits in with the set phrase

When you're writing a story, you should

- introduce the idea at the beginning of each paragraph (topic sentence) and then develop the idea
(eg **Three weeks ago, we got a leaflet in the post about a new department store in our town.** There was a special offer with about 25% off everything in the shop.
Mum and I had filled up our basket and we went to pay. We were really happy with how much we'd bought for the low price we would pay.
In the end, the bill came to £150 and Mum had just £120 in her purse! I told Mum not to worry and I showed the leaflet to the shop assistant with the discounts on everything we had bought.)
- make sure that the paragraphs are in a logical order
- end the story using the set phrase given without changing it

D Dorothy wrote a story that ends with the words '*It was the most disappointing day of my life!*'. Read her story and complete it with the sentences in the box.

> My friends told me that in that boutique, the prices were too high and that the quality wasn't any better.
> Finally, the night of the school dance arrived.
> I didn't like the idea of shopping from a catalogue though.
> A few months ago, my friends and I wanted to find something to wear to the school dance.
> When I walked in, I couldn't believe my eyes!
> My friend Sally had a catalogue at home, which she did most of her shopping from.

(1) .... We sat at Carrie's house and talked about what we could buy to wear and where we could buy it from. Everyone wanted something that was cheap but good quality.

(2) .... All my friends found something they liked in it and the prices were very low. (3) .... As the prices weren't high, I thought that the quality would be very bad and I wanted to buy something from the local boutique.

(4) .... I didn't believe them, so I went and bought a really expensive dress. I could see that it wasn't anything special, but it was from Marlene's boutique and everyone knew that.

(5) .... I couldn't wait to show my dress to everyone as I knew they wanted to see the dress I had spent so much money on. (6) .... Sally and I were wearing exactly the same dress in the same colour. It was the most disappointing day of my life!

Now it's your turn!

1 You are going to write a story about a shopping experience that ends with the words '*It was the most exciting day of my life.*' Use Arthur's writing plan to make notes for your story.

My writing plan notes

Paragraph 1: ....
Paragraph 2: ....
Paragraph 3: ....
Paragraph 4: ....

2 Now use your writing plan notes to write a story. Then copy your story onto the Writing Project page for Unit 9 on page 99.

10 Technology

A Match the words with the numbers on the picture.

calculator   cordless phone   headphones
keyboard   laptop   mobile phone   mouse
printer   screen   webcam

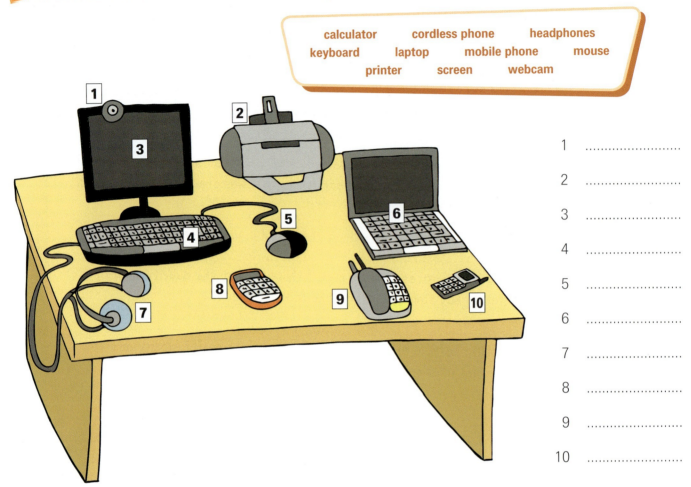

1 ....
2 ....
3 ....
4 ....
5 ....
6 ....
7 ....
8 ....
9 ....
10 ....

B Listen to an advertisement for a new mobile phone and complete the notes.

More than a mobile phone

Name: **(1)** ......Gotaphone......

Screen size: **(2)** .... inch

How to use: touch virtual **(3)** .... with fingers

Send: **(4)** .... and text messages

Free: set of **(5)** .... with a microphone

Use it as: **(6)** .... phone, video camera, TV, computer and MP3 player

58

C Listen to the six conversations and tick the correct answer for each one.

1 What did Richard buy?

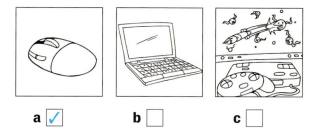

a ✓   b ☐   c ☐

4 What present did Shirley's brother give her?

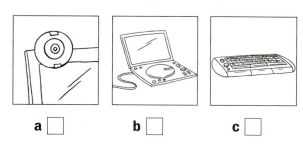

a ☐   b ☐   c ☐

2 What is Pauline doing?

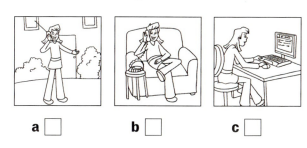

a ☐   b ☐   c ☐

5 What is Len taking back to the shop?

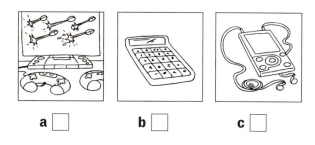

a ☐   b ☐   c ☐

3 What has Chris just bought?

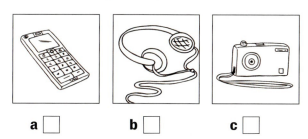

a ☐   b ☐   c ☐

6 How much does Nina pay for printer ink?

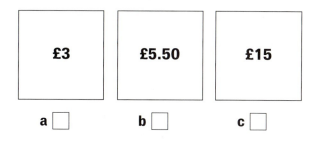

a ☐   b ☐   c ☐

Speaking

A Work with your partner to ask and answer these questions about computers.

Do you use a computer?

If so, what do you use it for? Where do you use it?

If not, would you like to use one? Why?/Why not?

Do you think young children should learn to use computers? Why?/Why not?

At what age do you think they should start learning?

B Ask and answer questions with your partner. Student A should turn to page 78 and look at cards 9A and 10A. Student B should turn to page 81 and look at cards 9B and 10B.

C Choose one of the objects below and describe it to your partner. Your partner must guess which object you have chosen.

1

4

2
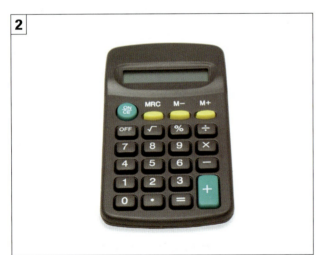

5

3

6

Writing

Unit 10

A Match the words with the descriptions.

1 calculator
2 webcam
3 screen
4 headphones
5 keyboard
6 mouse
7 DVD player
8 computer game

a Your friends can see you on their computers when you use this.
b You look at this to see the picture on a computer or TV.
c You can play this online or from a DVD.
d You put these on to listen to music without annoying other people.
e You can play films on this and watch them on a TV or computer.
f This has got letters and numbers on it for writing on a computer.
g You can open files and do many things on the computer with this.
h This helps you to do maths.

B Read Catherine's description of something she has lost and answer the questions.

Lost mobile phone

Yesterday, I lost my mobile phone. I realised that I didn't have it on my way home from university. The last time I remember seeing it was during the break at one o'clock when I finished eating lunch.

My phone is small and thin and it's got a pink cover. It's got quite a big screen and you can see the time on it and a picture of my dog, Toots. The phone's also got a camera, which I'd taken lots of photos with on a trip to Austria. The numbers on it are blue and silver. It's got blue headphones too, which I use to listen to music.

I'd like to get it back, as I've got some important numbers in it. So if you find a thin pink phone which has got a big screen with a picture of a dog on it, please hand it in at the university office or contact me at home and I'll arrange to collect it.

Thank you!
Catherine Carruthers, Class 10
Home number: 278541

1 Where was Catherine when she noticed that she had lost her phone?

....

2 When was the last time she saw her phone?

....

3 What did she have on her screen?

....

4 What colour are the numbers on her phone?

....

5 What else did she lose?

....

6 Why is it important for her to find her phone?

....

10

Read again!

In which paragraph does Catherine
1 describe her phone? ....
2 say why she wants to get her phone back? ....
3 say when she knew it was lost? ....
4 say what anyone who finds it should do? ....
5 say when she last had her phone? ....
6 say thank you and give her details? ....

Complete Catherine's writing plan

Title: ....
Paragraph 1: ....
Paragraph 2: ....
Paragraph 3: ....
Ending: ....

C Catherine used these phrases in her description. Find them and underline them.

> I remember seeing
> I finished eating
> I'd like to get
> I'll arrange to collect

Now complete the chart with the words in the box. Some words can go in both columns.

> enjoy   finish   hate   hope   learn   like   need   offer
> promise   remember   spend time   start   want   would like

-ing	Infinitive
....	....
....	....
....	....
....	....

62

D Read Jack's description of something he has lost and complete it with the verbs in backets in the correct form.

Lost laptop

Two days ago, I wanted (1) .... (go) and search the Web and I realised that I didn't have my laptop anymore. I had promised (2) .... (help) my friend in the library and that's the last time I remember (3) .... (have) my laptop.

My laptop is thin, it's silver on top and black underneath and it's got a big 19 inch screen. The keyboard inside is grey and the letters and numbers on it are black. I also had a mouse with my laptop when I last saw it, which was silver and black, too. I had many video games and photos on my laptop, but the most important thing is my work. I was doing a project for college, which I hadn't finished (4) .... (write).

I hope (5) .... (find) my laptop as I spend a lot of time every week (6) .... (work) on it and because I won't be able to buy a new one. If you see a silver laptop, which is black underneath, please contact me.

Thank you,
Jack Hobbs
Tel. 3289009

Now it's your turn!

1 Imagine that you have lost something. You are going to write a description of what you have lost to put on a noticeboard. Use Catherine's writing plan to make notes for your description.

My writing plan notes

Title: ....
Paragraph 1: ....
Paragraph 2: ....
Paragraph 3: ....
Ending: ....

2 Now use your writing plan notes to write a description to put on a noticeboard. Then copy your description onto the Writing Project page for Unit 10 on page 101.

11 Holidays and travel

🔊 Listening

A Complete the advertisements.

> bed and breakfast   cabin   flight   cruise   full board   half board
> package deal   resort   reservation   safari   self-catering   sightseeing

Let's Go Travel Agency

Exciting **(1)** .... !
Enjoy 8 nights in Kenya – flights, 4-star hotel with **(2)** ....
Breakfast and evening meal in our restaurant.

Skiing at a beautiful
(7) .... in Switzerland, three days in a wooden chalet with **(8)** ....
Special 20% discount if you make a
(9) .... before the end of this month.

Luxury **(3)** ....
around the exotic Caribbean islands with **(4)** ....
All meals served in our top quality restaurant. Sleep in an air-conditioned
(5) ....
Ship stops at islands for
(6) ....

Great **(10)** ....
to Ibiza. Direct
(11) ....
from Manchester, stay in a lovely villa. Price includes transport,
(12) ....
accommodation and a day trip around the island on a yacht.

64

B Listen to a woman asking for information about holidays in Africa and complete the notes.

Special offer!

Type of holiday: **(1)** ....Safari.... and beach

Package deal includes: **(2)** ...., transport to hotel, accommodation and the safari

Hotel is in: **(3)** ...., Kenya

Accommodation: Luxury hotel with **(4)** .... board

Cost of holiday: **(5)** £ .... per person

Reservation: Before **(6)** ....

C Listen to Sandra talking to her teacher about her holiday and circle a, b or c to complete the sentences.

1 Sandra and her family went
   a to France.
   b on a Mediterranean cruise.
   c to Portugal.

2 They went there
   a by boat.
   b by train.
   c by plane.

3 They stayed
   a in a hotel.
   b in a beautiful villa.
   c on the cruise ship.

4 The holiday was
   a expensive.
   b a package deal.
   c cheap.

5 Sandra's grandparents had a small
   a balcony.
   b cabin.
   c living room.

6 Sandra and her parents usually had dinner
   a on the cruise ship.
   b at a local restaurant.
   c at their hotel.

A Work with your partner to ask and answer these questions about holidays.

What time of year do you prefer to have a holiday?
Where do you usually go on holiday?
How do you like to travel?
Where do you usually stay?
What do you like to do on holiday?
Which was the best holiday you've ever had? Why?

B Work with your partner and decide which of these winter holidays you would like to go on.

Caribbean Dream!

Enjoy a cruise in the Caribbean and visit Grenada, with its colourful houses and national parks and Barbados, with its beautiful sandy beaches and clear waters. Flights and full board accommodation included. Price for seven days is £750 per person.

Skiing in wonderful Salzburg

Stay at this hotel, which is a large wooden chalet, and enjoy 7 days of skiing for £550 per person. Half board accommodation and travel included.

C If you could go anywhere, where would you go? Complete the notes about your ideal holiday. Then tell the class about it.

Where: ....

Who with: ....

Why: ....

How: ....

Accommodation: ....

Writing

A **Complete the chart with the words in the box.**

> beach   bed and breakfast   by plane   by ship   by train   cabin   chalet   cruise
> flight   full board   half board   hotel   safari   self-catering   skiing   villa

Type of holiday	Transport	Accommodation	
....	....	....	....
....	....	....	....
....	....	....	....
....	....	....	....

B **Read Beth's narrative about a journey and write *T* for true or *F* for false.**

A journey to remember

Last year, my family and I went to Greece. The day we left our house, I was so excited! Although it was cold and wet in England, I put on my summer clothes. We got into the taxi and we were driven to the airport.

Our flight left at nine in the morning and got to Athens at four in the afternoon. We had woken up early and I was very tired. As a result, I slept during the whole flight and I missed lunch! When we arrived, we were taken to the port to catch the boat to the island of Paros.

At the port, it was very windy and the boat didn't leave straightaway. Even though I had been on a boat before, I took some sweets with me, just in case I didn't feel well. One hour later, the boat left. My brother wanted to go outside. Although I felt ill, I agreed to go with him. As soon as I went outside, I felt terrible and I sat down. I couldn't find my sweets anywhere! I could see big waves and that's the last thing I remembered.

A few minutes later, I was lying down inside a cabin. My brother was laughing. I felt hungry, as I hadn't eaten all day, so Dad got me a sandwich. After I had eaten, I felt a lot better. However, I decided to stay inside for the rest of the journey!

1 Beth went to Greece two years ago. ....
2 They took their family car to the airport. ....
3 Beth and her family went to Paros by plane. ....
4 It was the first time Beth had been on a boat. ....
5 Beth felt ill when she went outside with her brother. ....
6 After Beth had eaten, she went outside again. ....

Read again!

In which paragraph does Beth talk about

1 her journey by plane? ....
2 what happened just before and after the boat left the port? ....
3 how she felt when she left home? ....
4 when she travelled, who she was travelling with and where to? ....
5 what happened in the end? ....
6 how the weather was when they set off from home? ....
7 how they got to the airport? ....
8 what happened when they arrived in Athens? ....

Complete Beth's writing plan

Title: ....
Paragraph 1: ....
Paragraph 2: ....
Paragraph 3: ....
Paragraph 4: ....

C Beth used the words below in her narrative. Find them and underline them. Then answer the questions.

> although   as a result   even though   however   in case   so

Which words are used

1 to show contrast? ...., ..., ...
2 to show a result? ...., ...
3 to show a purpose? ....

D Read Matthew's narrative and complete it with the words from C.

A train journey I'll never forget

Three weeks ago, it was my birthday and my parents took me somewhere special. On the day, we all woke up early to get the train to London.

(1) .... I had been to London many times, I was very excited. We caught the train at Leicester Station. There weren't many people on the train, **(2)** .... we could sit wherever we wanted and we all sat by the window. The journey passed quite quickly and we soon arrived at St. Pancras Station in London. Dad then told us we had to take a train to Waterloo station and I thought our journey would end there. **(3)** ...., I was in for a surprise!

At Waterloo Station, Mum told us to run, **(4)** .... we missed the next train! I began to wonder where we were going!

The train left the station and I started to feel very tired. **(5)** ...., I fell asleep. Three hours later, Mum woke me up and I could see lots of colourful buildings. 'Happy Birthday!' Mum and Dad shouted. We had arrived at the Disneyland resort in Paris!

Now it's your turn!

1 Use Beth's writing plan to make notes for your narrative about a journey you have made.

My writing plan notes

Title: ....
Paragraph 1: ....
Paragraph 2: ....
Paragraph 3: ....
Paragraph 4: ....

2 Now use your writing plan notes to write a narrative about a journey you have made. Then copy your narrative onto the Writing Project page for Unit 11 on page 103.

12 Ambitions

Listening

A Match the people with the jobs they want to do when they are older.

a
I hope to design the tallest building in the world.

b
I wish I were in charge of a cruise ship.

c
My ambition is to work for a newspaper or a magazine and to write articles.

d
I love chemistry and I wish I could discover a new medicine.

e
When I grow up, I'd like to design clothes.

f
I've always wanted to give people advice and work in court.

g
My ambition is to work on an aeroplane.

h
I'd like to explore ancient sites and discover more about the past.

1 archaeologist ....
2 architect ....
3 captain ....
4 fashion designer ....
5 flight attendant ....
6 lawyer ....
7 scientist ....
8 journalist ....

B Listen to a girl talking to her grandmother about the job she would like to do and complete the note.

My perfect job

Job: (1) flight attendant
Special skills: foreign (2) ....
Qualifications: (3) .... degree
Reason:
- travel to places like (4) .... and Rio de Janiero
- meet (5) .... people

Character: (6) .... , calm, patient

C Listen to Karen and her dad talking about people's ambitions and match the names with the jobs.

1 Karen   a lawyer
2 Elizabeth   b architect
3 Luke   c captain
4 Nicola   d fashion designer
5 Harry   e flight attendant
6 John   f chef
                 g scientist
                 h journalist

A Work with your partner to ask and answer these questions about your ambitions.

> What kind of job would you like to do in the future? Why?
> What subjects do you need to do well in at school?
> Will you need to go to university?
> What qualities do you need to do this job?
> What else will you need to do to achieve your ambitions?

B Ask and answer questions with your partner. Student A should turn to page 78 and look at cards 11A and 12A. Student B should turn to page 81 and look at cards 11B and 12B.

C Look at the information about two people's ambitions. Discuss the similarities and differences with your partner.

Steve's ambition

Job:	fashion designer
Qualifications:	university degree in art and design
Where:	in a studio
Why:	creative, artistic work
Who with:	top models
Clothes for work:	anything he likes
Salary:	good if he works hard

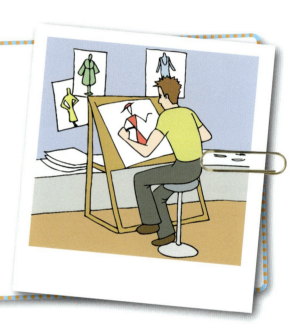

Tessa's ambition

Job:	lawyer
Qualifications:	university degree in law
Where:	in court
Why:	interesting work, likes to solve problems and help people
Who with:	people in trouble, police officers, judges
Clothes for work:	must be formally dressed
Salary:	well-paid

Writing

A Complete the crossword.

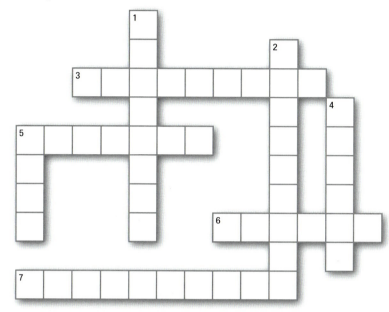

Across

3 Mike wants to be the .... who plans the best shopping centre in the world.
5 Jeff is a responsible man who would love to be .... of a ship.
6 Barry will be happy to be a .... in the local café.
7 Linda hopes people will read the articles she writes when she's a ....

Down

1 Susie's ambition is to work as a car ....
2 Wendy needs to study chemistry at university to be a ....
4 Kate would like to be a .... in court who helps honest people.
5 Sam cooks well and he wants to be a famous ....

B
Alex hopes to become a journalist and he has to choose which subjects to study at school next year. His parents want him to become an architect, just like both of them. He's afraid they may be angry with him and he needs their support. He wrote to his friend, John, asking for advice. Read John's reply and answer the questions.

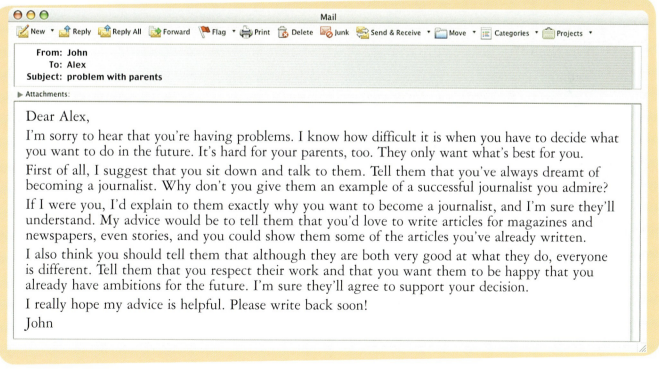

1 What does John think is difficult?
2 What does John think Alex should do first?
3 What has Alex always dreamt of becoming?
4 What would Alex like to write?
5 Why does John think Alex's parents will be happy?
6 What does John ask Alex to do at the end of his e-mail?

Read again!

In which paragraph does John

1. tell Alex to explain to his parents what he wants to be? ....
2. say what he would do in Alex's position? ....
3. say he's sorry Alex is having problems? ....
4. give a final piece of advice? ....
5. say he hopes he has helped and ask Alex to write back? ....
6. tell Alex his parents want what's best for him? ....
7. say Alex should explain why he wants to be a journalist? ....
8. give an example of someone who does this work? ....

Complete John's writing plan

Greeting: ....
Paragraph 1: ....
Paragraph 2: ....
Paragraph 3: ....
Paragraph 4: ....
Ending: ....
Sign off: ....

C John used these phrases in his e-mail. Find them and underline them. Then answer the questions.

> I'm sorry to hear that ...
> I suggest that ...
> If I were you, I'd ...
> I also think you should ...
> I really hope my advice is ...
> My advice would be ...
> Why don't you ...?
> You could ...

Which phrases are used

1. to end the e-mail? ....
2. to show understanding? ....
3. to give advice? ...., ..., ...
   ...., ..., ...

74

Unit 12

D Nicky is very upset. She's always dreamt of becoming a scientist, but her teacher has told her that next year she shouldn't study physics and chemistry, as she's much better at languages. She wrote to her friend, Caroline, asking for advice. Read Caroline's reply and complete it with the phrases from C.

From: Caroline
To: Nicky
Subject: problem with teacher

Dear Nicky,

(1) .... you're upset and you don't know what to do. It seems that your teacher is only trying to help you choose the subjects that you're best at, without thinking about what your ambitions for the future are.

First of all, (2) .... make an appointment to talk to the teacher. Tell him just how much you'd love to become a scientist, even though you aren't one of the best students in the physics and chemistry class.

(3) .... explain to him why you are interested in becoming a scientist. Talk about what kind of great scientific discoveries you'd like to make. (4) .... give an example of a famous scientist who didn't get good marks at school?

(5) .... you talk to your parents too. (6) .... to explain to them that even though you are better at languages, you still do well in science too.

(7) .... tell your parents and your teacher that, while you respect their opinions, you've made up your mind to try hard.

(8) .... useful. Please write back soon.

Caroline

Now it's your turn!

1 Imagine that your friend has sent you an e-mail asking for advice. His ambition is to become a mechanic, as he loves cars and he's good at fixing things, but his father wants him to go to university and study to become a lawyer. Use John's writing plan to make notes for your e-mail giving advice.

My writing plan notes

Greeting: ....
Paragraph 1: ....
Paragraph 2: ....
Paragraph 3: ....
Paragraph 4: ....
Ending: ....
Sign off: ....

2 Now use your writing plan notes to write an e-mail giving advice. Then copy your e-mail onto the Writing Project page for Unit 12 on page 105.

Speaking Cards

 **Learning** — CARD 1A

Look at the card and answer your partner's questions about this language school.

Sandleton Language School

Our beautiful school in the heart of the countryside offers three-month English courses. Lessons on Mondays, Wednesdays and Fridays.

For more information, call 321 45790.

 **Around town** — CARD 3A

Look at the card and answer your partner's questions about this town.

VISIT SWANPORT

- small town by the sea
- very quiet
- chemist's, florist's, baker's on the main road
- cinema, internet café, small park nearby
- very nice restaurant with sea view

 **Learning** — CARD 2A

Look at the card and ask your partner questions about a cookery course.

Hurst College cookery course

- address?
- how many students?
- how long/course?
- certificate?
- when/lessons?

 **Around town** — CARD 4A

Look at the card and ask your partner questions about a city.

City

- where?
- quiet/noisy?
- nearest shops?
- entertainment facilities?
- other buildings?

6 What's on? — CARD 5A

Look at the card and answer your partner's questions about this film.

ORION CINEMA

Exciting science-fiction film with a very good cast, an interesting plot and a very happy ending.

Friday–Sunday: 6.30 pm, 9.00 pm
Tickets: £6 for adults and £3 for children under twelve.

8 The natural world — CARD 7A

Look at the card and answer your partner's questions about this national park.

Kilimanjaro National Park

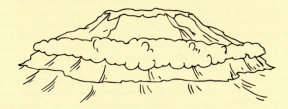

This national park is located in Tanzania, on Mount Kilimanjaro, the highest mountain in Africa. Visitors can climb to the icy peak of this dormant volcano, which has thick forests and semi-desert plants. The climb takes between five and eight days. Booking recommended in busiest months December and January.

6 What's on? — CARD 6A

Look at the card and ask your partner questions about a DVD shop.

DVD shop

- name?
- where?
- when/open?
- what kinds/films?
- cost?
- membership?

8 The natural world — CARD 8A

Look at the card and ask your partner questions about a national park.

National park

- name/park?
- where?
- how many/glaciers?
- wildlife?
- mountains/lakes?
- when/guided walk?

Speaking Cards

10 Technology — CARD 9A

Look at the card and answer your partner's questions about this computer.

Computer for sale

Desktop computer
only two years old
Large screen (17 inches)
Black with a matching keyboard
Comes with a white printer

A bargain at just £220
Mouse not included

12 Ambitions — CARD 11A

Look at the card and answer your partner's questions about this job.

PAOLO'S CAFE – WAITERS NEEDED

If you have some free time this summer and you'd like to earn some money, come inside! We're looking for part-time staff, every day from 6 pm to 10 pm, to start as soon as possible.

No experience necessary.
We pay £10 an hour.

10 Technology — CARD 10A

Look at the card and ask your partner questions about a special offer.

Special offer!

- what/for sale?
- colour?
- how old?
- camera?
- Internet?
- cost?

12 Ambitions — CARD 12A

Look at the card and ask your partner questions a job.

Job advertisement

- kind/job?
- where?
- qualifications?
- part-time/full-time?
- special ability?
- projects?

2 Learning — CARD 1B

Look at the card and ask your partner questions about an English course.

English courses

- name/school?
- countryside or city?
- when/lessons?
- how long/courses?
- telephone number?

4 Around town — CARD 3B

Look at the card and ask your partner questions about a town.

Town

- where?
- quiet/noisy?
- nearest shop?
- entertainment facilities?
- where/walk?

2 Learning — CARD 2B

Look at the card and answer your partner's questions about this cookery course.

Hurst College

31 Hurst Avenue

One-month cookery course.

Join us every Tuesday and Thursday.

Only 5 students in each class, so hurry!

Certificate for every student who finishes the course.

4 Around town — CARD 4B

Look at the card and answer your partner's questions about this city.

Visit Lumchester

- city centre
- busy, lively
- shops and offices everywhere, police station and hospital around the block
- newsagent's on the next block
- 2 cinemas, many cafes and a shopping centre, big park good for walks

Speaking Cards

 **What's on?**   CARD 5B

Look at the card and ask your partner questions about a film.

> **FILM**
>
> - TITLE?
> - WHERE/SEE FILM?
> - WHEN?
> - WHAT KIND/FILM?
> - PLOT?
> - CHILDREN'S TICKET? £?

 **The natural world**   CARD 7B

Look at the card and ask your partner questions about a national park.

> **National park**
>
> - name/park?
> - where?
> - booking necessary?
> - volcano/active?
> - what plants?
> - how many days/climb?

 **What's on?**   CARD 6B

Look at the card and answer your partner's questions about this DVD shop.

> **New shop now open at 24 Highland Road.**
>
>
>
> Membership for over 18's only.
> New DVDs £1.50 per day.
> Old favourites – DVDs or videos
> only £2.50 per week.
> Wide choice of films. All the best comedies,
> family dramas, adventures, thrillers,
> science fiction, romance.
>
> **Open every day 11 am – 10 pm.**

 **The natural world**   CARD 8B

Look at the card and answer your partner's questions about this national park.

> **Glacier National Park**
>
>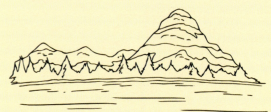
>
> Located in Montana, USA.
> More than 50 glaciers,
> huge mountains with snowy peaks and
> around 200 lakes.
> Visitors can also see black bears,
> mountain goats, wolves,
> deer and colourful wild flowers.
> Walking trips daily with experienced guides.

 **Technology** — **CARD 9B**

Look at the card and ask your partner questions about an item for sale.

For sale

- what/for sale?
- keyboard/printer?
- how big/screen?
- mouse?
- how old?
- cost?

 **My ambitions** — **CARD 11B**

Look at the card and ask your partner questions a job.

Job advertisement

- kind/job?
- experience needed?
- where?
- working hours?
- how much/earn?
- when/start?

 **Technology** — **CARD 10B**

Look at the card and answer your partner's questions about this mobile phone.

Special offer!

Great new mobile phone for sale
Fashionable phone with an orange cover and a colour screen

- Send text messages
- Take photos
- Surf the Internet

Special price: £82 with headphones, £75 without

 **My ambitions** — **CARD 12B**

Look at the card and answer your partner's questions about this job.

Architect wanted

Cumberfield Town Hall is looking for a young architect with a university degree in architecture. Must have special ability to design environmentally-friendly buildings.

Full-time work, office hours 9 am – 5 pm.

Major projects will include plans for new shopping complex.

1 Special people

Writing Project

From:
To:
Subject:
▶ Attachments:

 # 3 Homes

 *Writing Project*

4 Around town

Writing Project

Special events

Writing Project

8 The natural world

Writing Project

Shop till you drop!

Writing Project

10 Technology

Writing Project

Holidays and travel

Writing Project

Writing Project

Word list

Unit 1

admire (v)
appearance (n)
area (n)
arrive (v)
artist (n)
attractive (adj)
board game (n)
bring – brought – brought (v)
caring (adj)
casually (adv)
character (n)
choose – chose – chosen (v)
chubby (adj)
coach (n)
contrast (n)
creative (adj)
destroy (v)
dress (v)
earthquake (n)
education (n)
elderly (adj)
excellent (adj)
expect (v)
extremely (adv)
fashionably (adv)
forget – forgot – forgotten (v)
generous (adj)
good-looking (adj)
hard (adv)
helper (n)
honest (adj)
immediately (adv)
in danger
in his forties (exp)
in his teens (exp)
in his thirties (exp)
join (v)
joke (n)
keep – kept – kept (v)
lazy (adj)
middle-aged (adj)
organisation (n)
over (adv)
patient (adj)
postman (n)
prize (n)
quite (adv)
reason (n)
reliable (adj)
result (n)
ring – rang – rung (v)
share a secret (v)
shy (adj)
singer (n)
slim (adj)
sociable (adj)
sporty (adj)
succeed (v)
take care of (exp)
talented (adj)
talkative (adj)
thoughtful (adj)
train (v)
trust (v)
until (adv)
well-built (adj)
well-dressed (adj)
winner (n)

Unit 2

bright (adj)
certificate (n)
chemistry (n)
Chinese (n)
computer studies (n)
cookery (n)
detention (n)
during (prep)
enjoyable (adj)
exam (n)
final (adj)
French (n)
huge (adj)
library (n)
local (adj)
look forward to (exp)
mark (n)
naughty (adj)
nearby (adv)
noisy (adj)
paper (n)
part (n)
pass (v)
playing field (n)
pottery (n)
revision (n)
Spanish (n)
test (n)
university (n)
useful (adj)

107

Word list

Unit 3

antique (adj)
bungalow (n)
chalet (n)
chimney (n)
cottage (n)
cramped (adj)
decorate (v)
description (n)
feature (n)
fence (n)
fireplace (n)
for sale (exp)
furniture (n)
garage (n)
go with (phr v)
knock down (a building) (phr v)
line (n)
location (n)
main road (exp)
material (n)
modern (adj)
old-fashioned (adj)
opinion (n)
opposite (n)
origin (n)
peaceful (adj)
residential (adj)
roof (n)
rose (n)
round (adj)
semi-detached (adj)
shape (n)
size (n)
spacious (adj)
square (adj)
suburb (n)
terraced (adj)
tiny (adj)
view (n)
wall (n)

Unit 4

baker's (n)
bank (n)
block (n)
bowling alley (n)
bus stop (n)
car park (n)
cross (v)
entertainment (n)
facilities (pl n)
florist's (n)
hospital (n)
left (n)
miss (v)
newsagent's (n)
one-way street (exp)
pedestrian crossing (n)
petrol station (n)
police station (n)
right (n)
round (adv)
roundabout (n)
straight ahead (exp)
takeaway (n)
third (adj)
town hall (n)
traffic lights (n)
turning (n)

Unit 5

act (v)
activity (n)
arrange (v)
arrangements (pl n)
ballet (n)
be keen on (exp)
book (v)
canoeing (n)
chess (n)
cricket (n)
cycling (n)
drama (n)
golf (n)
hiking (n)
hotel (n)
ice skating (n)
indoor (adj)
instructor (n)
leisure (n)
outdoor (adj)
resort (n)
role (n)
scuba diving (n)
skateboarding (n)
speak – spoke – spoken (v)
stage (n)
studio (n)
water sport (n)
windsurfing (n)
yoga (n)

Unit 6

action (n)
action-packed (adj)
adventure (n)
alien (n)
brilliant (adj)
cappuccino (n)
cast (n)
comedy (n)
definitely (adv)
disappear (v)
ending (n)
entertaining (adj)
episode (n)
exotic (adj)
fall in love (exp)
famous (adj)
film (v)
follow (v)
footstep (n)
graduate (v)
in general (exp)
laugh (n)
mainly (adv)
middle (n)
miss (v)
plot (n)
predictable (n)
rent (n)
scene (n)
science-fiction (adj)
set – set – set (v)
soap opera (n)
southern (adj)
spaceship (n)
spaghetti (n)
square (n)
star (v)
storyline (n)
success (n)
surprising (adj)
team up (phr v)
thanks to (exp)
thriller (n)
unknown (adj)

Unit 7

amazing (adj)
atmosphere (n)
band (n)
bonfire (n)
carnival (n)
carry on
celebration (n)
charity (n)
come up to (phr v)
concert (n)
costume
crowded (adj)
dream – dreamt – dreamt (v)
event (n)
famous (adj)
fancy-dress (adj)
feel – felt – felt (v)
festival (n)
fireworks display (n)
full (adj)
go back (phr v)
Guy Fawkes Night (n)
magnificent (adj)
marathon (n)
mask (n)
medal (n)
notice (v)
out of this world (exp)
pick (v)
procession (n)
proud (adj)
raise money (exp)
scared (adj)
set out (phr v)
spectacular (adj)
suddenly (adv)
take a picture (exp)
take off (phr v)
take part in (phr v)
take place (phr v)
the Olympic Games (pl n)
the World Cup (n)
thousand (num)
tradition (n)
We couldn't believe our eyes! (exp)
wonder (v)
wonderful (adj)

Unit 8

active (adj)
bird watching (n)
break (n)
come out (phr v)

Word list

control (v)
deer (n)
desert (n)
discover (v)
dormant (adj)
erupt
extinct (adj)
glacier (n)
guided (adj)
golden eagle (n)
habitat (n)
ice (n)
important (adj)
kayaking (n)
lava (n)
mountain biking (n)
ocean (n)
peak (n)
plant (n)
point (n)
rainforest (n)
reach (v)
relaxation (n)
shell (n)
slope (n)
slow (adj)
smoke (n)
surface (n)
temperature (n)
the Atlantic (n)
the Pacific (n)
volcano (n)
whale (n)

wildlife (n)
wolf (n)

Unit 9

bargain (n)
boutique (n)
catalogue (n)
cucumber (n)
customer (n)
deliver (v)
department store (n)
designer clothes (exp)
develop (v)
disappointing (adj)
discount (n)
embarrassing (adj)
fit (v)
four-storey (adj)
grateful (adj)
greengrocer's (n)
jeweller's (n)
medium (adj)
necklace (n)
order (v)
shop (v)
price (n)
purse (n)
quality (n)
sales (n)
shopping complex (n)
tear – tore – torn (v)
till (adv)
web site (n)
worry (v)

Unit 10

calculator (n)
collect (v)
contact (v)
cordless phone (n)
cover (n)
hand in (phr v)
hate (v)
headphones (pl n)
ink (n)
keyboard (n)
laptop (n)
mobile phone (n)
mouse (n)
printer (n)
promise (v)
screen (n)
search (v)
the Web (n)
touch (v)
underneath (prep)
virtual (adj)
webcam (n)

Unit 11

accommodation (n)
air-conditioned (adj)
airport (n)
although (conj)
as a result (exp)
be in for (exp)
bed and breakfast (exp)
cabin (n)
cruise (n)

even though (conj)
flight (n)
full board (exp)
half board (exp)
however (conj)
in case (conj)
luxury (n)
package deal (exp)
purpose (n)
reservation (n)
safari (n)
self-catering (adj)
sightseeing (n)
straightaway (adv)
taxi (n)
villa (n)

wave (n)
yacht (n)

Unit 12

achieve (v)
advice (n)
ambition (n)
ancient (adj)
archaeologist (n)
architect (n)
be in charge of (exp)
be in trouble (exp)
captain (n)
chef (n)
court (n)
degree (n)
design (v)

fashion designer (n)
flight attendant (n)
formally (adv)
grow up (phr v)
journalist (n)
model (n)
past (n)
piece of advice (exp)
qualifications (pl n)
respect (v)
responsible (adj)
scientist (n)
site (n)
support (n)
support (v)
understanding (n)
well-paid (adj)

Abbreviations

n	noun	**adj**	adjective
pl n	plural noun	**adv**	adverb
v	verb	**conj**	conjunction
phr v	phrasal verb	**excl**	exclamation
prep	preposition	**exp**	expression
pron	pronoun	**num**	number
det	determiner		

Skills Booster 3
Alexandra Green

Copyright © 2008 Thomson Heinle, a part of
The Thomson Corporation. Thomson, the Star logo,
and Heinle are trademarks used herein under license.

All rights reserved. No part of this work covered by
the copyright hereon may be reproduced or used in
any form or by any means – graphic, electronic, or
mechanical, including photocopying, recording, taping,
Web distribution or information storage and retrieval
systems – without the written permission of the publisher.

For permission to use material from this text
or product, submit a request online at
http://www.thomsonrights.com

Any additional questions about permissions
can be submitted by email to
thomsonrights@thomson.com

ISBN-13: 978-960-403-557-1
ISBN-10: 960-403-557-6

Printed in Greece.
1 2 3 4 5 6 7 8 9 10   11 10 09 08 07

For more information contact Thomson Heinle,
High Holborn House, 50/51 Bedford Row, London WC1R 4LR, United Kingdom,
or you can visit our Internet site at elt.thomson.com

Acknowledgements
Project management by Liz Gardiner.
Recording and production at GFS-PRO Studio by George Flamouridis.
Illustrated by Katerina Chrysochoou.
Shakira photo for Unit 1 from Allstar Picture Library/Alamy.
Jackie Chan photo for Unit 1 from Pictorial Press Ltd/Alamy.